CW00549254

The Big Fix

The Big Fix

How South Africa Stole the World Cup

Ray Hartley

Jonathan Ball Publishers

Johannesburg and Cape Town

All rights reserved.
No part of this publication may be reproduced or transmitted,
in any form or by any means, without prior permission
from the publisher or copyright holder.

© Ray Hartley, 2016

Published in South Africa in 2016 by
JONATHAN BALL PUBLISHERS
A division of Media24 Limited
PO Box 33977
Jeppestown
2043

ISBN 978-1-86842-724-6
ebook ISBN 978-1-86842-725-3

Every effort has been made to trace the copyright holders and to obtain their
permission for the use of copyright material. The publishers apologise for any
errors or omissions and would be grateful to be notified of any corrections
that should be incorporated in future editions of this book.

Twitter: www.twitter.com/JonathanBallPub
Facebook: www.facebook.com/JonathanBallPublishers
Blog: http://jonathanball.bookslive.co.za/

Cover photo (Sepp Blatter and Chuck Blazer) by AFP Photo/Fabrice Coffrini
Cover by publicide
Design and typesetting by Triple M Design
Set in 10.75/18 pt Life Lt Std

Printed by *paarlmedia*, a division of Novus Holdings

To Sylvia, queen of words

Contents

Introduction

'Who could doubt that sport is a crucial window for the propagation of fair play and justice? After all, fair play is a value that is essential to sport.'

– Nelson Mandela

On 27 May 2015, at a luxury hotel in Switzerland, the unthinkable happened. The plush world of the Fédération Internationale de Football Association (Fifa) abruptly imploded. In an investigation led by the US Department of Justice, Swiss police officers arrested several top Fifa executives and raided their suites, taking away boxes of documents and computer hard drives in the most serious criminal action ever taken against a sporting body.

The indictment before a grand jury in New York named 14 officials involved in an elaborate global web of corruption, kickbacks, bribery and fraud. It detailed how the body that governed the beautiful game had been burrowed hollow from the inside by the worms who occupied several key executive positions.

Lucrative media and branding rights for Fifa's major tournaments had been bought with bribes paid through a string of foreign bank accounts in the US, Switzerland and the Caribbean. Officials had feasted on the sale of illicit tickets purloined from the governing body.

Presiding over all of this was Fifa's president, Sepp Blatter, a man deemed to be untouchable, who could arrange to see a head of state as easily as if he himself were the head of a major power. Blatter inhabited a world of unsurpassed luxury and privilege, ferried about in limousines from one flattering host to another as he presided over the distribution of the greatest prize in world football – the World Cup.

By the end of 2015, Blatter's executive team had been dismantled as, one by one, his loyal lieutenants had been stripped of their powers and given their marching orders. Among them was his closest aide, secretary-general Jérôme Valcke. Eventually, in December, Blatter himself fell victim to Fifa's ethics committee and was banished from the organisation's headquarters, in Zürich, from where he had ruled so ruthlessly.

Five years before this series of hitherto unimaginable events played out, Fifa had its last hurrah. Between 11 June and 11 July 2010, it held the World Cup tournament in South Africa.

And what a last hurrah it would be. When all the marketing spend, sponsorship and ticket sales had been tallied up, Fifa was richer than it had ever been, with over US$4 billion in the bank. Brazil's 2014 spectacle was yet to come, but by then Blatter would be a beaten man and the writing would be on the wall for Fifa's corrupt empire.

South Africa, it turned out, had been the perfect host country. Eager to please the world, it had more than bent over backwards for Blatter. Stadiums costing billions of rands had been constructed for the tournament, with little hope that they would ever recoup the money spent, never mind pay for their maintenance without taxpayer support. Huge swathes were cut through South African law as acts and amendments were shuffled through Parliament, exempting Fifa and its sponsors from tax obligations, from foreign currency regulations and even from the local competition law, ensuring that the Fifa entourage would vacuum up every loose dollar on offer before leaving town.

The South African people, crazy about football, spent their savings on tickets and thronged to stadiums, ensuring that even the most trivial match between the most inconsequential of teams would be played before a cheering full house.

It was a time of national fever. The South African flag was flown from car windows and draped over car mirrors. Office spaces were adorned with strings of multinational flags representing the competing countries. Every Friday, the nation became a sea of yellow as replica jerseys of the national team, Bafana Bafana, were worn. Grave warnings were issued that only official merchandise was to be purchased. There were dollars to be made from these strips for sportswear companies and the officials who rode on their coattails.

The opening game at Soccer City was the scene of almost religious fervour. The stadium, designed to look like a giant African calabash, had risen Phoenix-like from the ashes of the old stadium where Nelson Mandela had addressed the people of Soweto on 16 December 1990, after his release from prison. I remember the heat that day as we sat in the stands. His final line was: 'Gird your loins for the final assault. Victory is in sight! As a united people no force on earth can defeat us!'

After democracy was ushered in four years later, there was a return to international competition for South African sport, which had been isolated for many years because of apartheid. In 1996, I sat in the same stands to witness Bafana Bafana win the Africa Cup of Nations by defeating Tunisia 2–0.

On that opening day of the World Cup, played in a place so rich with history and before a people as free and loud as any in the world, football began its greatest party.

So exultant was the cheering and the blowing of vuvuzelas that when Bafana midfielder Siphiwe Tshabalala drove the ball into the corner of the net with a curving shot off his left boot, the stadium threatened to lift off the ground.

Even when Bafana were eliminated in the group stages – the first time that this had happened to a host country – the fervour remained undimmed. South Africans simply switched their support to Africa's most likely champions, Ghana. And when the Black Stars were eliminated by Uruguay in the quarterfinals, the fans looked for their favourite league and club stars and supported their teams.

In my case, it was a no-brainer. As an Arsenal supporter, I had to go with Spain because of Cesc Fàbregas, then still loyal to Arsène Wenger and the red and white strip.

I watched Spain beat Germany 1–0 at Durban's magnificent Moses Mabhida Stadium, its unique arch stretching high into the night sky as Carles Puyol headed home to secure Spain a place in the final.

Then came the final at Soccer City. Former president Nelson Mandela had missed the opening game due to a family tragedy – his great-granddaughter Zenani had died in a motor accident after the opening concert. But, to the surprise of the fans gathered in the stadium, Mandela took to the field before the final in a golf cart, waving at the near-hysterical fans and beaming his trademark smile. For an old man mourning the death of his great-granddaughter and beginning to be plagued by the illnesses that would bring about his end, it must have been an enormous act of will to brave the chilly temperatures. It was to be the last occasion on which the public he adored – and which adored him – would see him in person.

The final was a bad-tempered affair. One red card was issued, but there could have been several more if the referee had applied the law properly. Eventually the artful dodger, Andrés Iniesta, secured Spain's place in history with a goal in extra time.

The celebrations were loud and went on into the night.

And then the players, the foreign fans, the legions of reporters and the Fifa bigwigs left town and South Africans, who had been on their best behaviour for a month, returned to their normal ways.

The question that South Africans asked most frequently was why the organisation, efficiency and good cheer displayed by government, business and the people during the hosting of the tournament could not be applied to solving the country's pressing problems – getting water and electricity to the people, creating jobs and cutting down crime. The answers given were that we had a clear mission with clear timeframes, that there was national consensus and that we were being closely watched by Big Brother, Fifa, which would brook no slacking.

The World Cup, it seemed, had been a golden moment for the country, a special time when things had worked and we had done ourselves proud.

After the party, as they say, comes the hangover.

Hardly was the tournament over than the ruling party, the ANC, announced a clampdown on the media with a new 'media tribunal' to replace the self-regulation of the press and a 'Protection of Information Bill', which proposed to protect a wide range of information labelled 'security' and prevent its publication.

It was telling that the announcements, contained in a discussion document, were timed for after the departure of thousands of international journalists, who had filed thousands of reports mostly praising the way in which the World Cup had been organised.

No mention had been made of media controls during the thousands of hours of interviews on global television networks or in the thousands of column centimetres of coverage during the tournament, but then it all came out.

The discussion document read: 'Freedom of expression needs to be defended but freedom of expression can also be a refuge for journalist scoundrels, to hide mediocrity and glorify truly unprofessional conduct. Freedom of expression means that there should be objective reporting and analysis which is not coloured by prejudice and self interest.'[1]

Of course, all of this was being done in the interests of saving the press from itself: 'The tendency of dismissing any criticism of the media as an attack on press freedom results in the media behaving like a protection racket and leaves no space for introspection. For its own credibility, and in order to be at the forefront of determining the agenda for change and not against change, we have a responsibility to assist the media to shape up.'[2]

The tribunal idea would eventually be placed on the back burner, but only after the press agreed to tougher self-regulation. The worst aspects of the law aiming to protect information were altered after months of high-profile campaigning by civil society.

Crime, which had hit an all-time low during the tournament, spiked again as criminals sought to make up for lost time. The national police commissioner was found to have signed off on the procurement of new offices without following procedure and was eventually dismissed.

Imagine the shock, then, when the World Cup's dirty laundry began to pile up. The May 2015 Fifa indictment included a section that described how South Africa had bribed its way to hosting the tournament, paying Caribbean football supremo Jack Warner for three crucial votes, which turned out to be the difference between winning and losing.

The South African government and local football officials strongly denied the charges. There are several chapters of this book dedicated to trying to establish exactly what happened. It is a tale worthy of a thriller, with bank accounts in the Cayman Islands, secret emails and corporate intrigue in the corridors of the grand hotels of Zürich.

More dirty laundry came in the form of business collusion around the stadium contracts. It turns out that secret meetings were held to divide these contracts up among the big construction firms, and the exact profit margin each would earn was calculated and agreed on.

Then came revelations that the games played during Bafana Bafana's mercurial run prior to the tournament had been fixed by an Asian syndicate, which had somehow managed to persuade the national football association to use its referees. They proceeded to blow their whistles as often as their paymasters demanded, awarding dodgy penalties and even, on one occasion, insisting that a penalty be retaken when it was missed.

Behind all of this lurked a great human tragedy. In Mpumalanga, a council official who blew the whistle on corruption related to the building of a World Cup stadium had been gunned down in 2009. Pieces of an elaborate jigsaw puzzle of fraud and thuggery would be found in the years after the World Cup, pointing to more tender-rigging and an attempt to rob a community of its land without compensation.

When World Cup fever was at its height, stories critical of some aspects of the event were published, but they were overshadowed by the 'good news' story of progress in meeting the demands of Fifa and the economic boom that the tournament was supposed to ignite.

In 2010, I became editor of South Africa's largest newspaper, the *Sunday Times*. We published stories exposing hit squads and corruption around stadium tenders, but these stories were drowned out by the clarion call from government, business and civil society to 'get behind the World Cup', and for the nation to show the world its best side. As the national fervour grew, it became almost treasonous to question the World Cup. It was seen as the media's duty to support the staging of the event, helping to spread the word that the 'Afro-pessimists' were wrong and that an African country would put on a great tournament.

Stories raising awkward questions simply didn't get off the ground. They were sometimes seen as evidence that the press was not 'patriotic'. What dominated was the coverage of milestones, of the release of the World Cup mascot and of the great countdown. I was determined to tell, one day, the full story of this glorious but flawed event.

Years later, in December 2013, I found myself once more on the hallowed ground of Soccer City. This time there was no celebration. The good and the great had gathered to bid farewell to Nelson Mandela. It was an awkward moment for the nation.

Amid the solemn orations delivered by the likes of US President Barack Obama and the UN's Ban Ki-Moon, the crowd was restless, especially when President Jacob Zuma made his appearance. He was booed.

How had it come to this? How had the beautiful green turf of the World Cup, where Siphiwe Tshabalala had fired home his epic goal three and half years before, become the staging ground for a divided country tired of its leadership and angry at the state of the nation?

It occurred to me that what we had witnessed in 2010 was the grandest of illusions. We had projected ourselves as a united nation with an efficient and effective government. The truth was that we were fractured and unable to confront the massive challenges of poverty and unemployment.

This book represents my effort to understand what really happened when we put on the greatest show on earth. It is never easy to challenge the conventional wisdom, to cast doubt on certainties and to shine a light on the dark spaces where the truth is hidden.

As the layers of tinsel are stripped away from the World Cup, the somewhat less glamorous truth begins to show itself.

There is the glorious game of football with its stars on display, dazzling the world with a great sporting spectacle. But when you peek behind the World Cup curtain, your senses are astounded. Crawling about in shiny suits are every species of corruption, graft and greed imaginable as money is siphoned off the sport's fanbase to feed the game's elite.

Nobody can take away the joy, the celebration and the hope that was born when the World Cup came to South Africa. But we need to remember that it happened despite the greed, vanity and callousness of politicians and football administrators who saw it as just another feeding ground.

CHAPTER 1

A whistleblower sings

'You and I were buddies on the street and we agreed to sell
marijuana and we meant it. We were going to go into the marijuana
business. We committed the crime of conspiracy to distribute
marijuana, whether we ever distributed a single gram.'

– Judge Raymond Dearie

It was a cold November morning in Brooklyn, New York, in 2013. In
the United States District Court on Cadman Plaza East – an imposing
glass and concrete structure – Judge Raymond Dearie was presiding.
On his bench was a docket marked 13-MC-1011.

Grey-haired and with blue eyes that had seen it all before, he was
about to start the ball rolling on a story that would rock the world of
football to its core.

Before him was a motion to seal proceedings in a case that had
been years in the making. Driven by the US Attorney for the Eastern
District of New York, Loretta Lynch, the motion sought to seal a plea
bargain, making all but those in the courtroom privy to its secrets.

Lynch's representative before the judge was Assistant US Attorney
Evan Norris. Representing the defendant was attorney Eric Corngold.

Dearie, then 69 years old, was a former head of the District Court in the Eastern District. Ronald Reagan had appointed him to the bench in 1986. Now edging towards retirement, he had relinquished his job as head of the court to serve as one of its senior judges.

After identifying the small band of clerks and attorneys before him, he said: 'Somewhat to my surprise – but perhaps the situation will be corrected momentarily – we are in an empty courtroom although a very public courtroom.'[1]

He went on: 'For the record other than court personnel, pre-trial, my law clerk and the Court Security Officer, and the representatives of the US Attorney's Office, the Court Reporter, and my staff we are otherwise alone in this public courtroom.'

Dearie looked up at Norris and Corngold and ordered that the minutes of the hearing be sealed, authorising two copies – one for the government and another for Corngold. He ordered 'the safeguarding of all or any computers or other Court Reporter source material relative to the preparation of these minutes'.

The matter was one demanding high security – perhaps as high as the day Dearie had heard the guilty plea of Najibullah Zazi, an al-Qaida member who admitted in February 2010 to planning bombings on the New York subway system.

Dearie continued: 'I find that a public proceeding in this matter including but not limited to the identification of the defendant, would severely if not irreparably prejudice an ongoing investigation by the United States Attorney's Office and presumably the Grand Jury sitting here in the Eastern District of New York.'

The sealing of the yet-to-be-written record secured, Dearie turned to his clerk: 'Elie, seal the courtroom.'

Elie replied: 'Judge Dearie, the courtroom is locked.'

An afterthought struck the judge: 'Was it locked before I made the findings?'

The court security officer replied: 'I did, your Honor.'

Dearie had one more request: 'Will you do me a favor and just open the door, and see if there is anybody lurking about in the hallway yearning to get in here.'

While the security officer went to check the hallway, Judge Dearie squinted into the empty room and muttered, 'Monday morning at 10 after 10 – you would think we are in the middle of the night.'

The hallway was empty and the courtroom was sealed.

The judge said: 'That brings us to Mr Blazer.'

At that point, Charles 'Chuck' Blazer entered the courtroom from the secure area reserved for the accused. Although confined to a wheel-chair, he was still a large, imposing presence. Not for nothing had he earned the nickname 'The Belly' from an investigative journalist. And by the time he had finished testifying, his other nickname – 'Mr Ten Percent' – would make perfect sense.

Blazer did not have the opportunity to furnish the court with his full biography. If he had, he might have told of how his journey to the apex of American soccer had begun when his six-year-old son, Jason, had joined a soccer team in New Rochelle, New York.

As his son moved up the team ladder, Chuck Blazer became increasingly involved. Blazer made his fortune early as the owner of the business that manufactured the yellow, 'smiley-face' button that took off in the early 1970s.

At the age of 27 he cashed in his stake in the business, earning enough to enter a state of early retirement. He spent more and more time hanging around soccer and became a junior coach.

A photograph that Blazer liked to show visitors to his office in later years showed him as a trim young football coach, staring into the middle distance with hope and confidence.

Blazer's big break came in 1990 when his friend Jack Warner, who had just become the head of Concacaf – the football federation governing North and Central America and the Caribbean – appointed him general secretary.

The two built an empire on the back of bribery, extortion and money laundering, and by the time Blazer agreed to cooperate with the authorities he had foreign bank accounts and two Trump Tower apartments overlooking New York's Central Park.[2]

Blazer was living the life and he wanted the world to know it. He published a blog with the title 'Travels with Chuck Blazer and his Friends ...' in which he documented his brushes with the rich and famous.

There were pictures of Blazer with Nelson Mandela, with Prince William, and with any other famous person he could attach himself to, but most frequently, there were pictures of Blazer with Jack Warner, sitting somberly at some or other Caribbean football board meeting or at a press conference.

It goes without saying that the blog painted a rosy picture. Blazer was giving of himself to foster the beautiful game, enduring tedious meetings and the like with good cheer because the cause of football was a worthy one.

Then, one November evening in 2011, Blazer – by now morbidly obese – was driving his mobility scooter to New York's exclusive Elaine's restaurant when he was confronted by agents from the Internal Revenue Service (IRS) and the Federal Bureau of Investigation (FBI).

He had a choice: he could cooperate with their investigation into money that he had illicitly moved in and out of the US banking system, or they would cuff him and book him. Blazer had no choice but to concede that the game was up.

Back in the Brooklyn courtroom, Blazer and Dearie exchanged greetings. Blazer raised his right hand and was sworn in. Then Dearie explained in painful detail the agreement that had been reached under which Blazer would relinquish an appearance before the grand jury and enter a guilty plea.

Dearie then set about putting Blazer at ease.

Dearie: 'Let me begin first of all, sir, by asking you to state your full name.'

Blazer: 'Charles Gordon Blazer.'

Dearie: 'How old are you, sir?'

Blazer: '68.'

Dearie: 'You are the second person I know, I being the first one, to actually stop on that question. I guess it is some kind of Freudian block.'

Blazer: 'It is'.

The exchange set the tone. Blazer was cooperating and there was no need for hostility.

Blazer told Dearie his education had taken him partially through graduate school in New York.

His health was poor – worse than poor. By then wheelchair-bound, Blazer suffered from colon cancer for which he had undergone 20 weeks of chemotherapy. He tried to put a gloss on it by stating: 'I am looking pretty good for that. I am now in the process of radiation, and the prognosis is good.'

There were other ailments – Type 2 diabetes, coronary artery disease. Again Blazer tried to be cheery saying he was 'holding up reasonably well'.

This was not the whole truth. Blazer was by now a shadow of his former self. In his prime, he had been a bold, large-bodied man who dominated any room he entered with his physical presence, his thick curly grey hair framing a bearded face. In those days, his smiling eyes staring over his spectacles, he came across as a perspiration-beaded Father Christmas who had spent the night in a club and got lucky.

Dearie responded to Blazer's account of his health with 'good luck'.

The court's copy of Blazer's 19-page typed account was placed before him.

Dearie: 'The first question, did you read it?'

Blazer: 'Yes, I have.'

Dearie: 'Did you read it carefully?'

Blazer: 'Yes, I did.'

Dearie: 'Would you agree that this is an important 19 pages in your life right now?'

Blazer: 'Extremely so.'

Finally, the doors closed, the minutes sealed and the courtroom empty but for the essential players, it began.

Dearie: 'There are ten charges, if I am not mistaken, ten charges in total ...'

Blazer: 'That is correct.'

Dearie: 'The charges related to events involving an exchange of [illicit] payments for one purpose or another. They identify Fifa and its attendant or related constituent organization as what we call an enterprise, a RICO enterprise.'

RICO, Judge Dearie informed Blazer, was an acronym for Racketeer Influenced and Corrupt Organization. That was how football's governing body was being described on this winter's morning.

The charges, said Dearie, alleged 'a conspiracy to corrupt this enterprise through the anticipated payment of funds pursuant to various criminal schemes'.

Dearie then asked Blazer: 'Tell me what your understanding of a conspiracy is, what is a conspiracy?'

Blazer replied: 'That it is an activity conducted by a group of people for a specific aim and objective.'

Dearie adopted a schoolteacher's posture: 'That is a B-Plus.' He explained: 'It is an agreement to do something that the law forbids.'

Blazer replied: 'Okay.'

Dearie searched for a metaphor. 'You and I were buddies on the street and we agreed to sell marijuana and we meant it. We were going to go into the marijuana business. We committed the crime of conspiracy to distribute marijuana, whether we ever distributed a single gram. It is an agreement itself. Any questions about that?'

Blazer replied: 'No, sir.' He listened as Dearie explained that the charges included money laundering, tax evasion and the violation of financial reporting laws.

For each of counts one and two, racketeering conspiracy, Blazer could face 20 years in prison or a fine of up to US$250 000. Count three – money laundering – could result in a further 20-year sentence or a fine of US$500 000. Counts four to nine, for tax evasion, each carried a maximum term of five years in jail. Count 10, the failure to file information on foreign bank accounts, carried a potential ten-year sentence or a fine of US$500 000. If given the maximum sentences to run consecutively, Blazer would spend 100 years in jail – the rest of his life, a very uncomfortable prospect for a very ill man who loved his freedom.

Finally, Dearie asked: 'Are you ready to plead?'

Blazer: 'I am.'

Dearie: 'What is your plea to Count One through Ten inclusive, guilty or not guilty?'

Blazer: 'Guilty.'

Dearie: 'Mr Blazer, tell me what you did.'

In clipped legal language, Blazer told how he had been employed by Fifa and Concacaf: 'From 1997 through 2013, I served as a Fifa executive committee member. One of my responsibilities in that role was participating in the selection of host countries for the World Cup.'

The full extent of Blazer's involvement in the corruption of 'the enterprise' was placed on the record in a voice familiar with reading legal contracts.

'I agreed with other persons in or around 1992 to facilitate the acceptance of a bribe in conjunction with the selection of the host nation for the 1998 World Cup. Beginning in or about 1993 and continuing through the early 2000s, I and others agreed to accept bribes and kickbacks in conjunction with the broadcast and other rights to the 1996, 1998, 2000, 2002, and 2003 Gold Cups.' (The Gold Cup is a regional tournament held every two years and organised by Concacaf.)

'Beginning in or around 2004 and continuing through 2011, I and others on the Fifa executive committee agreed to accept bribes in conjunction with the selection of South Africa as the host nation for the 2010 World Cup.'

He continued, explaining how he had used email, telephone and wire transactions in a scheme to defraud Concacaf and Fifa, and how money had been illegally shifted from the US to the Caribbean and in the opposite direction: 'I agreed to and took these actions to, among other things, promote and conceal my receipt of bribes and kickbacks. I knew that the funds involved were the proceeds of an unlawful bribe.'

He had failed to pay tax or to file tax returns; he had run an illegal bank account in the Bahamas.

Dearie rounded off proceedings: 'I find that the defendant is acting voluntarily, that he fully understands his rights, the consequences and the possible consequences of his pleas, and there are a factual basis [*sic*] for these pleas of guilty. I therefore accept the plea of guilty to

Counts One through Ten inclusive of the information bearing docket 13-CR-602.'

It was 11 am. The courtroom emptied.

* * *

Once Blazer had been 'flipped' and had agreed to cooperate, he began to collect information for the authorities. Continuing with his Fifa duties, he helped the FBI build their case.

The FBI issued him with a keychain containing a tiny microphone that Blazer took with him to the London Olympics. He placed the keychain on a nearby table while entertaining visitors and chewing the fat over various corrupt schemes.[3]

On the same day that Chuck Blazer agreed to cooperate with the US authorities, across the world in Geneva, Fifa president Sepp Blatter had just won a minor victory. A Swiss initiative to cap top executives' pay had just failed. He called a press conference to announce that he was fighting match-fixing. He was blissfully unaware that a senior judge in a US courtroom had just described the body he had ruled for 17 years with an iron fist as a Racketeer Influenced and Corrupt Organization. He did not know that it was the beginning of the fall of Fifa's house of cards.

CHAPTER 2

The 2006 bid: So this is how it works

'On the opening day of the World Cup, Germans should dedicate
the games to Charlie Dempsey of New Zealand. More than any
other man, Charlie assured the hosts that this day would finally
come. Interestingly, enough, Charlie didn't do it by casting his vote
for Germany six years ago; rather he succeeded by not voting at all.'

– Chuck Blazer

Only eight countries have ever won the World Cup – Brazil (5 times),
Germany (4), Italy (4), Argentina (2), Uruguay (2), France (1),
England (1) and Spain (1) – reflecting the total domination of Europe
and South America over the sport. For the 60 years between the first
World Cup, in 1930, and the 1990 edition, a European or a Latin
American country had hosted the tournament.

In 1994, the cosy tradition was broken when the United States
staged the event. Fifa took firm aim at the lucrative US market,
with its massive television revenues and sponsorship money. The
move was richly rewarded. Despite the fact that the US lacked a

quality national soccer league, new attendance records were set as Americans piled into stadiums at an average of 69 000 spectators per game. Unsurprisingly, South America and Europe dominated the competition, with Brazil beating Italy in a penalty shoot-out in the final.

But the face of the competition had changed forever. From now on, Fifa would seek to make it a 'global game'. In exchange, it was hoping for a much larger global television audience that would generate higher revenue from the sale of media and branding rights.

South Africa's then football boss, Solomon 'Stix' Morewa, returned from watching the US tournament determined to take advantage of Fifa's global ambitions by getting South Africa on to the Fifa map as a host nation. He wrote to Fifa offering the country as a host.

Morewa would eventually be dragged down by scandal after the Pickard Commission of Inquiry (1996) found that he had presided over financial mismanagement. But back then 'Bra Stix' was the mover and shaker in local football. He had been at the helm of the South African Football Association (Safa) when it hit its all-time peak in 1996. That year, South Africa hosted the Africa Cup of Nations as a late replacement for Kenya.

The year before, South Africa had hosted the Rugby World Cup and the national team, the Springboks, had beaten the All Blacks at Ellis Park in the final. On that occasion, Nelson Mandela won over white South Africa by taking to the field in captain François Pienaar's number six jersey before the game. Rugby had become an entrenched part of white South African culture, and Mandela's appearance was a deeply symbolic act of reconciliation.

By contrast, football was the sport of black South Africa, with massive radio and television audiences following the local league, dominated by the Soweto giants Orlando Pirates and Kaizer Chiefs and Pretoria's Mamelodi Sundowns.

The national team, recently dubbed 'Bafana Bafana' – the boys – was new to international football. At home that year, they were to prove a formidable side under coach Clive 'The Dog' Barker.

In the first round, they demolished the fancied Cameroon 3–0 and beat Angola 1–0 before losing a dead rubber to another continental superpower, Egypt, by a solitary goal.

In the quarterfinals they faced another continental giant in Algeria, winning a tight game 2–1. In the semifinal they demolished Ghana 3–0 to book their place in the final against Tunisia.

It was as if it had all been scripted. Nelson Mandela took to the FNB Stadium in Bafana captain Neil Tovey's jersey before the game, and what had become known as the 'Madiba magic' worked again as South Africa won the tournament 2–0. Striker Mark Williams came off the substitutes' bench to score both goals.

After the trophy presentation, Mandela and Tovey raised the cup together, a carbon copy of the image from a year earlier when Mandela and Pienaar had done the same with the rugby trophy.

There was a sense that South Africa's stars were aligning.

More than that, it was a bold statement that South Africa was a serious footballing nation. If it was to host a World Cup, it would not only be because of its substantial infrastructural advantages over other African competitors but also because it could justly claim it was the continent's best on the field.

The door had opened to a previously unthinkable African hosting of the World Cup and Fifa took note.

The idea of a South African bid now had real momentum, and with Mandela in its corner, how could it lose? In 1997, the country established the South Africa 2006 World Cup Bid Committee. A 46-year-old MP of the ruling African National Congress (ANC), Danny Jordaan, was asked to head it up.

Intelligent, articulate and understated, Jordaan had a long history in the struggle for racially integrated sport. He had played cricket and football in an era when strict racial segregation applied. Jordaan had been a frontline activist in the fight against apartheid and against segregated sport.

Jordaan came from Port Elizabeth in the country's Eastern Cape province – a region known more for its rugby than its football. He joined the militant Black Consciousness student movement, the South African Students' Organisation (Saso), which had been founded by Steve Biko, who was to die after brutal torture while being held in detention by the security police. Nine of Saso's leaders would be sentenced to up to ten years' imprisonment on Robben Island, where Nelson Mandela and other ANC leaders were being held.

Jordaan was also a member of the South African Council on Sport, which actively sought to have South Africa's whites-only sports teams excluded from international competition under the slogan 'No normal sport in an abnormal society'. Under apartheid, only white South Africans represented the country in international sport, although this was amended in later years to allow a limited number of black participants. Apartheid ensured that whites were well financed and enjoyed the best facilities.

Jordaan, along with many other leading Black Consciousness activists, shifted his allegiance to the banned and underground ANC and the United Democratic Front, a broad coalition of student, civic and religious bodies that acted as the ANC's internal front. The ANC disagreed with Biko's Black Consciousness doctrine, embracing a more inclusive non-racialism, a policy that was to become epitomised by Nelson Mandela's reconciliation policies.

Jordaan rose to prominence in the party's regional structures and when Mandela's party won the first democratic election in 1994, he became an MP in the first truly representative South African parliament.

In 1997, Jordaan gave up his seat to head up the football association and the 2006 bid committee. It was not his first foray into the politics of international sport. He had served as a director on the failed bid by the City of Cape Town to secure the 2004 Olympic Games.

The 2006 bid, blessed by Nelson Mandela and with the backing of Fifa's Sepp Blatter, who was painfully aware of the importance of Africa's 54 votes in presidential elections, seemed like a sure thing.

Jordaan and his committee worked the 24 members who would make the decision hard, quietly confident that the Fifa decision to award the tournament to new continents and the backing of Blatter would seal the deal.

Bid committee officials travelled the globe, visiting the heads of regional associations to present the South African case. They were welcomed and allowed to make their pitch by all but one of the six continental regions.

The regional exception was Oceania, which consisted chiefly of island nations where football was not a major sport. Countries such as New Zealand, Fiji, Tonga and Samoa were rugby powerhouses. Oceania's top-ranked football team – New Zealand – occupied the 150th position in Fifa's rankings in February 2016.[1] Nonetheless, Oceania was awarded a seat on the Fifa executive that would decide on which nation would host the World Cup tournament in 1996.

Charles 'Charlie' Dempsey had run the Oceania Football Confederation (OFC) since 1982. He had made the Queen's birthday honours list in that year as a Commander of the Order of the British Empire (CBE). Dempsey's crowning achievement had been to guide Soccer New Zealand to an unlikely berth at the 1982 World Cup finals in Spain.

The undisputed patriarch of soccer in Oceania took up the Oceania seat on the Fifa executive in 1996.

An official close to the 2006 bid told me how it was simply impossible to get a meeting with Dempsey, who said his mind was made up and he wasn't interested in hearing the South African case.

Dempsey was determined to vote for England and that was that.

The South Africans eventually arrived unannounced at his offices and, after some toing-and-froing, were able to make a presentation to him. He remained staunchly loyal to the English cause, however, and made it plain that they had wasted their time.

'He was one of those old colonial types who turned his nose up at us,' said one of those who tried to persuade him.

When July 2000 rolled around, the South Africans had done their sums and they knew that Dempsey's vote was the key. They had managed a minor coup, persuading the Oceania region that, in the event that England dropped out of the running, Dempsey would switch his vote to South Africa in the following round.

The committee assembled in Zürich, Switzerland, to make the final decision.

Five countries were in the running until Brazil dropped out on the eve of voting. That left South Africa, Germany, England and Morocco still in contention.

It soon became apparent that the voting would be tighter than antici-pated. In the first round, Germany received ten votes to South Africa's six, England's five and Morocco's three. Morocco was eliminated, and in the second round of voting, Germany and South Africa both edged up to 11. England, with just two votes, was out.

The contest now came down to a straight contest between Germany and South Africa.

In the event of a tie, Blatter would have the casting vote and his commitment to an African tournament made it a racing certainty that he would lean South Africa's way.

David Will of Scotland would switch from England to Germany. Tight though the race was, South Africa was confident that Oceania would come good. It had, after all, mandated Dempsey to vote for South Africa once England was eliminated. But this was a dog-eat-dog race and the pressure on Dempsey to vote for Germany was extraordinary.

Germany wanted the World Cup badly. It was prepared to alter its global diplomatic stance if necessary. On the eve of the commit-tee's meeting, German Chancellor Gerhard Schröder lifted an arms embargo on Saudi Arabia, a decision that would later be exposed by the German media as an inducement for that country to support the German bid. A consignment of rocket-propelled grenades was delivered as proof of Germany's changed attitude.[2] Germany's *Die Zeit* newspaper revealed that the lifting of the embargo ahead of the vote was done at the behest of the German Football Association. It also reported that German industrial behemoths Bayer and Volkswagen offered Thailand and South Korea increased investment in exchange for their backing.

On the evening of 5 July 2000, Dempsey was to experience this pressure at first hand. First came a hoax bribe request from the Frankfurt-based German satirical magazine, *Titanic*, which put a card under his door offering him a cuckoo clock and a Black Forest ham if he switched his support to Germany.

Then came the real pressure, which Dempsey would later say reached 'intolerable' levels. He answered his phone to discover that it was none other than the great Nelson Mandela on the line, asking him to vote for South Africa.

But it was an altogether more sinister intervention that pushed Dempsey over the edge. Years later, Dempsey would reveal that he had been threatened by what he described as 'influential European interests', who indicated that there would be 'adverse effects' for the OFC if he did not vote for Germany.

'The night before the Fifa meeting, I received a number of calls which disturbed me, one of them was a threatening call. It had also been made clear to me by influential European interests that if I cast my vote in favour of South Africa there would be adverse effects for OFC in Fifa.'[3]

By the next morning, Dempsey had made his mind up. He had a bombshell for the executive committee ahead of the final round of voting, telling the assembled members that he had a statement to make. Botswana official Ismail Bhamjee later recalled: 'He said he had been accused of bribery and corruption and would not vote again after England were out. The Committee were totally dumbstruck.'[4]

Dempsey's decision to abstain gave the hosting of the tournament to Germany by 12 votes to 11, with Sepp Blatter not being called on to provide the casting vote.

The South Africans were furious. Jordaan said: 'Why Dempsey decided not to participate in the final voting is beyond me. In the end it was a matter of that single vote he withheld which made the difference. It would have been better if he had cast his ballot for Germany and we had lost 13–11.'[5]

The officials of the Oceania region held a four-hour meeting to find out how their mandate to vote for South Africa had been ignored, and then forced Dempsey to step down as president two years ahead of his contract expiring.

Dempsey was quoted as saying after his resignation: 'Behind closed doors the executive met and discussed – I wasn't present – and gave approval to the explanations that I gave for what took place in Zürich.

'But after all this consideration and the [media] harassment I will retire at the end of September because I cannot accept what has taken place over the last three days.'[6]

Exactly what transpired in the weeks and months leading up to the finalisation of the 2006 bid is not known in full.

Twelve years later, in July 2012, Blatter finally spoke out about the affair. Controversy had just erupted over the selection of Russia to host the 2018 tournament and Qatar for 2022: 'World Cups being purchased ... I am reminded of the World Cup allotment for 2006, when someone left the room at the last moment. And instead of 10–10 [Blatter's memory had faded, the tied vote would have been 12–12] the vote was suddenly 10–9 in favour of Germany ... Perhaps in that situation I was also too well-meaning and naïve.'[7]

The British investigative journalist Andrew Jennings took a less flattering view of Blatter's role in the loss of the 2006 bid: 'Africa had been assured by Blatter it could expect to win. That was a problem – Mandela would get the shaft but hey! no worries, the old man didn't have a vote at Fifa.'[8]

Jennings reveals how three crucial players – the former football star Franz Beckenbauer, TV mogul Leo Kirch and go-between Fedor Radmann – were the authors of a devious plan to ensure that Germany won the hosting rights, with Blatter's tacit approval.

'Germany, with its tight financial regulation, experienced anti-fraud detectives and determination to control ticket allocations, was not the first choice for some ExCo members. South Africa offered lax supervision, a growing post-apartheid culture of public corruption – and photos with Nelson Mandela to show off to friends, family and neighbours.'[9]

Early in 2000, the three realised that their bid was in trouble, as South Africa's pitch, spearheaded by Nelson Mandela, appeared to be winning the day. The financial consequences for Kirch, who stood to make billions of euros out of the broadcasting rights, were high.

Beckenbauer was, 'helpfully', chairman of Bayern Munich, the club he had both played for and managed. 'They had been busy negotiating rights to some surprising football matches for a team of Bayern's immense status. They would play Malta's national team and there would be an extraordinary fee of US$300 000 for the TV rights, to be paid by KirchMedia into an undisclosed bank account in Malta. The president of Malta football, Joe Mifsud, was a member of Fifa's ExCo.'[10]

Another big fee was paid for Bayern to play Thailand in Bangkok and another for Bayern to play the Trinidad national team: 'The president of Trinidad football, Jack Warner, was a member of Fifa's ExCo – and known as a man who even holds out his hand in his sleep. The match never took place, but a year later Warner was given Caribbean TV rights to the 2002 and 2006 World Cups. The price was 4.8 million Swiss francs but it is unlikely Warner ever paid.'[11]

Beckenbauer was prepared to do whatever it took to win the bid. Incredibly, Bayern travelled to Tunis to play the top local team, Espérance. 'A bonus for the foreign teams was that Bayern would pay all their own expenses. In total KirchMedia was prepared to spend a budget of 3.5 million euros to win it for Germany. Why spend this money? German analysts estimated that in 2006 KirchMedia could make an additional profit of 500 million Swiss francs if the tournament was played in Germany.'[12]

According to Jennings, as the intrigue intensified, it became apparent that Germany could find itself with the executive split in a 12–12 draw. That would leave Blatter with the casting vote. He had publicly committed himself to supporting the South African bid and would have to honour this, not least because breaking his word would cost him the African bloc vote in the approaching 2002 Fifa presidential election. 'Blatter would be the ultimate winner, winning the UEFA votes, sympathizing with the African losers and making them promises for the future.'[13]

When it all came down to Charlie Dempsey, Germany turned the screws and he buckled, pulling out of the voting altogether.

Jennings is sceptical about Dempsey's claim that he had been intimidated into pulling out. 'Charlie dodged reporters as best he could but when cornered, babbled about "intolerable pressure".' This must have been intense. Charlie was now an old man but he had emigrated from a tough area of Glasgow at the age of 30 and built a successful construction business in New Zealand. What had intimidated this bare-knuckle, in-your-face, old-fashioned street fighter?

'It was a massive scandal; nobody outside Fifa believed Dempsey. He had only one function at the Fifa meeting: to cast a vote. Now he was sure to be thrown out of the Oceania presidency along with his daughter, Josephine King, who he had appointed as his general secretary in 1988. Because he was terrified by a cuckoo clock, a parcel of sausages and a call from Mandela? There was something deep and dirty going on here.'[14]

Jennings notes that, in the many years since the vote, neither Blatter nor any other member of the executive have publicly criticised Dempsey for walking out at the crucial moment.

'It's tempting to think this is another manifestation of the criminal enterprise created by [former Fifa president João] Havelange and maintained by Blatter. The crooks do crooked things; the others, well-rewarded to leave Blatter to run Fifa any way he chooses, avert their eyes and seal their lips.'[15]

Three weeks after the vote, at the August meeting of the Fifa executive, confidential minutes obtained by Jennings read: 'The Fifa president expressed regret that the outcry in the wake of the election had forced

Charles Dempsey to hand in his resignation from the Fifa Executive Committee and the OFC presidency and that he had answered Charles Dempsey's letter of resignation on 15 July by assuring him that the Executive Committee would in due course seek a way to recompense him for his long and loyal services to Fifa.'[16]

In 2004, Dempsey received his Fifa Order of Merit.

Chuck Blazer paid tribute to Dempsey at the German World Cup in 2006: 'On the opening day of the World Cup, Germans should dedicate the games to Charlie Dempsey of New Zealand. More than any other man, Charlie assured the hosts that this day would finally come. Interestingly, enough, Charlie didn't do it by casting his vote for Germany six years ago; rather he succeeded by not voting at all.'[17]

Blazer went to say that for Dempsey, switching his vote to South Africa 'would be like breaking marriage vows' to Europe. 'Europe did support Oceania becoming a Confederation and Charlie wasn't one who forgot his friends.'[18]

Years later, in October 2015, the German news magazine *Der Spiegel* would add another twist to the plot. It claimed its reporters had seen documents showing that the sportswear company Adidas had made a donation of 10.3 million Swiss francs to the German bid committee, which had not appeared on its books.

The money was used 'to secure the four votes belonging to the Asian representatives on the 24-person Fifa executive committee'.[19] The report continued: '*Spiegel* has learned that the decision to award the 2006 World Cup to Germany was likely bought in the form of bribes. The German bidding committee set up a slush fund that was filled secretly by then-Adidas CEO Robert Louis-Dreyfus to the tune of 10.3m Swiss francs.'[20]

In a shock to the German football fraternity, the magazine revealed that national hero Franz Beckenbauer, who headed the bid committee, and the head of the German Football Federation, Wolfgang Niersbach, 'were aware of the fund by 2005 at the latest'.[21]

When Louis-Dreyfus called in his secret loan, 'internal documents show that a cover was created with the help of global football organising body Fifa to facilitate the payment'.[22]

The cover was a gala Fifa opening ceremony to which the Germans made a financial contribution. The gala was cancelled and the money was moved from a Fifa account in Geneva to one belonging to Louis-Dreyfus.

For Danny Jordaan and his team, the 2006 defeat had been a bitter pill to swallow. The 'support' of Sepp Blatter and Nelson Mandela had been defeated by greed and graft. There were, apparently, no guarantees in this World Cup bidding game. Perhaps things would have to be done differently next time. Perhaps it was time to roll up the sleeves and play by the unwritten rules.

CHAPTER 3

2010: Victory at all costs

'Whatever South Africa's president told those two men in that room, it must have been extremely powerful, because they stayed true to their promise.'

– Jermaine Craig

When the dust had settled on the failed 2006 bid, there was disappointment and heartbreak. But it was not long before the bidding machine, bruised by the last-minute defeat but not broken, chugged back into life.

Fifa's Sepp Blatter, a beady eye on the leadership election to be held at the 2002 Fifa Congress, swung into action. He knew that the last-minute gazumping of the South African bid by Germany beggared belief. It was feeding the growing public view of Fifa as an association where bribery and behind-the-scenes dealings were more important than fair play.

A month after the meeting to allocate the 2006 bid, on 3 August 2000, Fifa's executive committee met again and, with an uncharacteristic swiftness, decided there and then on 'the principle of World Cup rotation'. This policy would see to it that from now on a different continent would stage each iteration of the World Cup, making good on Fifa's promise to take the game to all corners of the globe. This was ratified at its congress in Zürich two days later.[1]

Then, to further tilt the playing field in South Africa's favour, Fifa's executive decided in March 2001 that by 'rotation' it meant that the next Cup had to take place on African soil. Just over a year later, in October 2002, Fifa sent a circular to its African members inviting them to submit bids.

South Africa, sensing that its time had finally come, was the first to declare its interest, followed by Morocco, Libya, Egypt, Nigeria and Tunisia.

South Africa compiled a bid book in which it argued its case for the tournament. It opened with a letter from then President Thabo Mbeki, who went out of his way to impress: 'As the national Government, we unequivocally commit ourselves to provide every guarantee requested and every resource necessary to assure the Fifa executive committee of our ability to provide Africa's Stage in 2010 for a highly successful, prestigious international series of events.'[2]

Mbeki was effectively signing a blank cheque – one which FIFA would not hesitate to cash.

It was not often that Mbeki, a brooding intellectual given to questioning the commercial motives of global entities, was driven to this sort of hyperbole. But winning the World Cup required supplication to the Fifa machinery by even the most independent-minded of government leaders.

With the advantage of many years of hindsight, the South African bid book seems almost quaint in its modesty. It was the bid of a developing country conscious of its limited means.

It proposed that the major centres of Johannesburg, Cape Town and

Durban would simply upgrade existing rugby and football stadiums to World Cup standards. Durban's King's Park stadium was described as the perfect venue for that city. It was 'the prime sporting venue' in the city. All that would have to be done to bring the stadium up to World Cup standard would be the addition of upper tiers at the north and south ends of the ground to create 'a fully encircled oval with a new net capacity of 60000 seats'. The stadium would be good enough to host a semifinal. Among its attractions was its proximity to Durban International Airport, which was close to the city.

In Cape Town, another rugby stadium, the 'cherished' Newlands, was identified as the perfect venue. It would be a simple matter of converting two standing areas to seating and installing modern communication infrastructure for the stadium to reach the required standard.

It was a bid in keeping with Mbeki's oft-repeated refrain of 'fiscal discipline'. Wherever possible, existing infrastructure would be repurposed, and only when there was no alternative would money be spent on building new stadiums.

It was a commitment that would soon be broken, but for now, South Africa was on course to impress Fifa with a relatively modest plan.

In November 2003, a body called the 'Fifa Inspection Group' arrived in South Africa to evaluate the bid. Chaired by Jan Peeters, the president of the Royal Belgian Football Association, the group spent a week visiting proposed venues and talking to officials in government and in football, with the aim of discovering how well prepared South Africa would be to put on the tournament in 2010.

They were impressed with what they saw, and South Africa clearly emerged as their preferred choice, although they made an effort to make it seem that there was continental competition from Egypt and Morocco.

The executive summary on South Africa's bid said it was apparent that a successful bid 'will generate significant unity among the different ethnic groups that were separated socially, culturally and in sport for years'.[3]

The visitors were impressed with South Africa's many 'world class cultural and tourist attractions'.

It was a ringing endorsement that must have made the members of the South African bid committee believe they were just a few short steps from securing the 2010 hosting rights. The bid was described as 'clear, detailed and stable, proving its reliability. Furthermore, there is a strong backing for the bid from the Government. The population is very enthusiastic about football, spontaneously showing their joy at the prospect of hosting the World Cup. Despite questions about security in the country, the legacy compared to the investment needed will be a great contribution to the country.'[4]

South Africa was placed in number one position. The most critical sentence came at the end of the summary: 'The Inspection Group's opinion is that South Africa has the potential to organise an excellent World Cup.'[5]

The use of the adjective 'excellent', placing South Africa ahead of Egypt ('very good'), Morocco ('very good'), Tunisia ('good') and Libya ('great difficulties'), was telling. The choice was, at this point in the process, a no-brainer.

The detailed country section did include a worrying question: 'It is extremely difficult for the Inspection Group to be able to assess all the figures submitted. It was, however, not possible to check how these budget estimates were reached, nor was it possible to understand fully the philosophy behind them all.'[6]

The committee was, however, satisfied with one crucial requirement that it had of all bidding nations: 'The South African Government has pledged a full guarantee that no taxes would be levied on participants in the 2010 Fifa World Cup™. Legal advisers at Fifa have checked these documents and given their agreement to them.'[7]

The South African bid team knew that the approval of a Fifa structure – or even of its president, Sepp Blatter – was no guarantee of victory. Once again they did all they could to persuade the six continental federations: AFC (Asia), Caf (Africa), Concacaf (North and Central America and the Caribbean), Conmebol (South America), OFC (Oceania) and UEFA (Europe).

On 14 and 15 May 2004, Fifa's executive committee met in Zürich to decide who would host the 2010 World Cup.

There would be one last chance for bidding countries to make their pitch.

By now, most of the Fifa members had made up their minds. Some believed it was South Africa's turn and that the great Nelson Mandela should not again suffer the ignominy of another stolen bid.

But it soon became apparent that the South Africans still faced a tough challenge. Morocco might have scored lower in the bid evaluation process but somehow it had managed to win the support of many of the executives.

Back in 2000, Charles Dempsey had been the fly in the ointment.

This time around it was clear that it was the delegates from Concacaf whose votes remained uncommitted.

The awkwardly named Confederation of North, Central American and Caribbean Association Football (Concacaf) was an altogether greater threat than Oceania had been. It boasted two countries that had already hosted the World Cup – Mexico, which had done so twice, and the USA.

Presiding over Concacaf was another patriarch of world football, Austin 'Jack' Warner.

A history teacher and sometime politician in his home country of Trinidad and Tobago, where he had been an MP, Warner had ruled the roost with an iron rod since 1991. Warner was also in charge of the football association of Trinidad and Tobago and of the regional body, the Caribbean Football Union.

Warner had never been one to pass up the opportunity to make a fast buck, and both Concacaf and the Trinidad association rented offices in properties that he owned. The properties were part of a multi-million dollar real estate empire that could not be explained by the salary he received for his official duties.

In 2002, Warner had been exposed for selling World Cup tickets in an illegal scheme, something for which he received a slap on the wrist from Blatter, who remained painfully conscious of the regional federation's voting rights. At Fifa presidential elections, each member country had the same vote and Concacaf's archipelago of footballing countries controlled no fewer than 35 votes. Tiny islands such as St Kitts and Nevis or Grenada had as much say in Blatter's future as footballing giants such as Germany or Argentina. The region was second only to Africa when it came to the number of votes in Fifa presidential elections. Concacaf also held three of the 14 votes on the executive committee that would decide the 2010 World Cup host nation.

Somehow, South Africa would have to get Warner and his colleagues on board. The bid CEO, Danny Jordaan, described these three votes as the difference between success and failure for the South African bid. 'By April [2004], a consensus emerged that the contest would be won in North and Central America. I agreed. We needed to secure three votes from Concacaf, the swing region, to win,' said Jordaan.[8]

The South Africans had gone out of their way to woo Warner and his fellow Concacaf voters. In one of the less edifying spectacles of the bid process, Nelson Mandela was persuaded to come out of retirement from public life to take a long flight to Trinidad where, on 5 April 2004, he and Archbishop Desmond Tutu conducted a meet and greet with Warner and tried to get his vote. Warner relished the photo opportunity but still would not commit to the bid.

Mandela would be dragged out of retirement again to lobby Fifa executives ahead of their decision on the 2010 host nation in May 2004.

On the morning before Fifa was to make its decision, Mandela and Mbeki met with Warner and fellow Concacaf executive Charles Blazer – also a member of the Fifa executive – at the Dolder Grand Hotel in Zürich, where Mandela was staying.

Warner brought Mandela a gift of two 'Madiba shirts'.

Journalist Jermaine Craig, who would later become a member of South Africa's World Cup organising committee team, wrote: 'In the privacy of Mandela's room Warner assured Madiba of Concacaf's "full support" in Saturday's election ... He promised Mandela that he, the

American Blazer and Costa Rica's [Isaac] Sasso would back South Africa.'[9] Craig wrote that Mbeki then held a further private meeting with Blazer and Warner, 'ordering everyone out of his room when doing so, even his closest personal aides'.[10]

'Whatever South Africa's president told those two men in that room, it must have been extremely powerful, because they stayed true to their promise' to support the South African bid, Craig wrote.

Former BBC sports editor Mihir Bose, who interviewed Warner immediately after that meeting, wrote in his 2011 book, *The Spirit of the Game: How Sport Made the Modern World*, 'What these men discussed has never been revealed, but I caught up with Warner in the corridor immediately after the meeting. When I asked him who was going to win – Morocco or South Africa – he said, "who knows, anything can happen". Then he gave a big smile, suggesting that the Mandela trump card had worked.'[11]

Bose wrote: 'For Mandela, the man who is nearest to a modern-day Gandhi, to be forced to "schmooze" Warner shows that when your country wants the World Cup, you have to take any road you can. The trick here is to pretend you are on a high road talking of how well-equipped you are to hold the World Cup and all the good it will do for the country and the world. But the real journey is along the low road, making deals with Fifa executive members.'[12]

Craig continued: 'After Mandela and Mbeki's meeting with Warner and Blazer the mood changed considerably in the South African camp. Tense, anxious faces were replaced by smiling, more relaxed ones as they felt a bit more secure in the belief that they had secured the crucial Concacaf votes.'[13]

On 14 May 2004, the day before the vote, President Thabo Mbeki addressed the Fifa executive committee. It was, supposedly, one last effort to convince them why they should vote for South Africa and not Morocco as the host of World Cup 2010.

Mbeki, who had made the 'African Renaissance' the centrepiece of his foreign policy, focused the address on Africa. 'I am also privileged to convey to you our deep felt gratitude for giving the peoples of Africa the possibility to host the Soccer World Cup. The historic decision you took has made the unequivocal statement that you, the leaders of world soccer, are firmly of the view that Africa's time has come!'[14] he said.

'Today and tomorrow, the eyes of 800 million Africans will be focused on Fifa House, Zürich. It is true that each one of these Africans will be waiting in tense expectation to see which among our sister countries will have the privilege to host the 2010 Soccer World Cup.'[15]

Mbeki was careful to include the African diaspora – a reference to the island nations of Jack Warner's Caribbean empire – in his vision: 'Through this decision, you conveyed the message to all Africans, both on the continent and the African Diaspora, that you are ready and willing to accompany us on our journey of hope, and give us the strength and stamina we need to traverse the difficult terrain that separates us from Africa's renaissance.'[16]

Mbeki referred to the high-powered figures behind the South African bid, saying: 'the delegation appearing before you includes the President of the South African Football Association, the leadership of our Bid Committee and other South African soccer leaders, three of our Nobel Peace Prize Winners, three of the most outstanding African footballers, business leaders, Ministers of our government and, of course, the President of our Republic.'[17]

The three Nobel prize winners he referred to were Mandela, former President FW de Klerk and Archbishop Desmond Tutu, who were members of the South African delegation along with footballers George Weah and Gary Mabbutt.

He pledged that 'if South Africa is granted the privilege to host the 2010 Soccer World Cup, we will ensure that we respect the high standards that Fifa must necessarily set as a condition for granting this privilege.'[18]

Mbeki went so far as to thank Blatter – who had attended the country's celebration of the first decade of democracy three weeks earlier – for his role in bringing about democratic change in South Africa, saying: 'We were greatly honoured that you were able to attend these historic celebrations because as Africans and South Africans, we had wanted to say – thank you Fifa for what you did to help us achieve our freedom!'[19]

He finished his speech with: 'We pray that thus you will help us fully to restore Africa's dignity, as humanity advances to the year 2010, the end of the first decade of the 21st century and the third millennium, as together we undertake a journey of hope that would be crowned by the joyful festival that will be the 2010 Soccer World Cup.'[20]

By that afternoon, the South Africans were certain of victory. Journalist Andrew Donaldson, who was in Zürich to cover the decision, described the scene: '… celebrations at the upmarket Dolder Grand Hotel, where the South Africans were staying, began the day before the winner was announced.

'The party started on the afternoon of Friday, May 14 2004,

immediately after the last presentation to Fifa. The national propensity for the copious and conspicuous consumption of alcohol was proudly on display. Small Swiss serving folk recoiled, as if from vipers, as large men in Bafana Bafana merchandise bore down on the bar like Visigoths and waved empty beer glasses, demanding they be filled – to the brim – with scotch.'[21]

The party continued into the night. That evening, South Africa threw its grand banquet, which was attended by Mbeki as well as Mandela, De Klerk and Tutu. Perhaps more significantly, the banquet was graced by Warner's wife, Maureen.[22]

What is clear is that Warner changed his mind at the last minute. In the weeks leading up to the 2010 host nation vote, he was backing Morocco.

A few weeks before the vote, he invited fellow Fifa executive Ahongalu Fusimalohi, of Tonga, to his suite at the Savoy Baur en Ville Hotel in Zürich. During their 15-minute conversation, Warner made it clear to Fusimalohi that he was supporting Morocco 'because the North African country needed the tournament to lift it out of poverty'.[23]

A report by the Bloomberg news agency said: 'During their hotel-suite chat, Fusimalohi said he humoured Warner by saying he would reconsider his vote, but didn't change his mind. On returning to his room to get his jacket before joining his wife and son for dinner, the Tongan official found a note slipped under the door.

'The anonymous note said a vote for Morocco to organise the World Cup "stood to benefit him by 150K," according to his recollection.'[24]

Fusimalohi said: 'I just tore it up and threw it in the rubbish bin, I never even told my wife.'[25]

But, on the day of the vote, Warner told Fusimalohi that he was now backing South Africa. According to the Bloomberg report, Fusimalohi said: 'Warner made no mention of why he switched sides.'[26]

Five African countries – Tunisia, Libya, Morocco, Egypt and South Africa – had been in the running to host the tournament. Tunisia withdrew from the race a week before the vote. The Libyan bid was excluded for political reasons; Libyan leader Muammar Gaddafi would not allow a team from Israel to play on his country's soil should the bid succeed.

That left South Africa, Morocco and Egypt. It ought to have been a shoo-in for South Africa, which had been rated more highly by the inspection team and offered a far better tourism and sporting infra-structure. But, incredibly, it was a tight-run affair.

Memories of Charles Dempsey's last-minute withdrawal from the voting for the 2006 World Cup host were fresh in the minds of the South Africans. Some believed that South Africa's high crime rate and the HIV/Aids pandemic would count against the country. And then there was the uncertainty over Warner and his friends.[27]

After one round of voting, South Africa emerged victorious, winning by 14 votes to Morocco's 10. Egypt received no votes. As predicted, Warner had been the kingmaker.

The three swing votes pledged to Mandela and Mbeki by Warner the day before had made the difference between South Africa winning or losing the vote. If they had gone the other way, Morocco would have won 13-11.

Jermaine Craig wrote that the final vote showed that Warner and his two colleagues 'were indeed the "key" factor in Saturday's outcome.'[28]

On 15 May 2004, Blatter finally ended the suspense. Taking to the stage for one of Fifa's most-watched rituals, he opened a white envelope and then said: 'The 2010 Fifa World Cup will be organised in South Africa.'[29]

'We can all applaud Africa. The victor is football. The victor is Africa,'[30] he said.

Mandela could not control his tears. 'I feel like a young man,' said the 85-year-old statesman.

His first words were for the losing bidders: 'And the beauty of this victory is that we were dealing with highly capable competitors which made it difficult for us to forecast what the result was going to be.

'You must not be discouraged. It is no reflection of your efforts. Next time when you compete, you may be luckier,' he said.

'South Africans,' he said, 'should treat this decision with humility and without arrogance because we are, after all, equal.'[31]

Mandela returned to the Fifa decision to boycott South Africa following the Soweto uprising of 1976: 'It is 28 years since Fifa took a stand against racially divided football and helped to inspire the final story against apartheid. While we were on Robben Island, the only access to the World Cup was on radio. Football was the only joy to prisoners.'[32]

Local Organising Committee CEO Danny Jordaan was ecstatic: 'It was a moment I will never forget for the rest of my life, along with the release from prison of Nelson Mandela. It was a release of emotions, joy and pain, of years of sitting at airports, on the road, on taxis and trains, going to houses and knocking on the doors of members of the Fifa executive committee.'[33]

Tutu, who had also travelled to the event, did what he did best – he cracked a joke: 'I promise to buy all Fifa executives first-class tickets to heaven. But first I shall go outside and dance.'[34]

For the moment, it seemed that the persuasive powers of Mbeki and Mandela had swayed Warner, persuading him to take the high ground and dump Morocco for South Africa.

But there was much more to it. Warner, it turns out, had not changed his spots. He had switched sides for altogether less honourable reasons. It would take more than a decade for the truth to come out, and, when it did, it would shake South Africa and the football world to their foundations.

CHAPTER 4

What's US$10 million between friends?

'At one point, Warner also directed Co-Conspirator #14 to fly to Paris, France, and accept a briefcase containing bundles of US currency in US$10 000 stacks in a hotel room from Co-Conspirator #15, a high-ranking South African bid committee official.'

– US Attorney General's indictment

By September of 2007, three years had passed since the right to host the World Cup had been awarded to South Africa. The cranes on the skylines of the major cities attested to the building of new stadiums. The highways of Johannesburg were undergoing renewal on a scale not seen in decades as the transport infrastructure demanded by the World Cup was put into place.

But while South Africa was steaming ahead with its hosting plans, out across the Atlantic Ocean, Jack Warner wanted his money.

It had been three years since the South Africans had promised him US$10 million for the 'development of football' in the Caribbean. Neither Warner nor the South Africans had issued any public statement about the promise. The amount of US$10 million had never been announced or mentioned in any of the tens of thousands of words issued in the publicity ahead of the tournament.

If no one had found out about the promise, Warner reckoned, enough time had passed since the 2004 vote on the South African bid for the payment to be made without raising eyebrows.

Warner went all the way to the top, letting Sepp Blatter know that he was an unhappy man – an unhappy man who presided over a federation with 35 votes at a Fifa congress where Blatter wished to be re-elected.

In Chuck Blazer's plea bargain testimony, he talked of how he would bug Warner periodically about the money. Warner and Blazer must have been like two mosquitoes buzzing around Blatter's ears, going on and on about the money they had been promised.

Finally, in September 2007, Blatter could take the whining no more. He turned to his right-hand man, Fifa secretary-general Jérôme Valcke, to sort it out before it became a headache.

Valcke had a chequered history in Fifa. He was fired as the organisation's marketing director in December 2006 for his role in sponsorship negotiations with Visa and MasterCard. A New York judge found he had lied to both parties.[1] The court said that the contract between Fifa and Visa was invalid because MasterCard had not been given the right of first refusal as a long-time sponsor. This was 'anything but fair play'.

Fifa's condemnation of Valcke was brutal. 'Fifa's negotiations breached its business principles. Fifa cannot possibly accept such conduct among its own employees.'[2]

But, astonishingly, in October of 2007, Valcke was re-employed as Fifa secretary-general, causing London's *Independent* newspaper to comment in a headline, 'He scored the worst-ever own goal. Now he's running football'.[3]

Valcke's return to the top echelons of Blatter's administration is a complicated tale, which is described in the *Independent* article: 'Valcke's fortunes began to change in May when an appeals court panel vacated the original judgment and remanded the case. Less than a month later, on 21 June, Fifa and MasterCard reached agreement to terminate legal proceedings at a cost to Fifa of $90m (£45m), including settlement of a separate marketing dispute. Within six days of that, Valcke was back – this time as general secretary.'

Valcke told the newspaper: 'I made the biggest mistake of my life by saying that in business we don't always say the truth and you could describe that as a commercial lie. And then I was dead. The day I [used the phrase] "commercial lie", I was out – completely destroyed by [MasterCard's] lawyer.

'I won't say that in the same situation I would do the same today, but I don't have the feeling we have been so dirty.'

Valcke added: 'Whatever Blatter asked me, and what I committed to deliver when I joined Fifa, I did. So we have a strong relationship, Blatter and myself.'[4]

Valcke went on to make a startling admission: 'The old world was the system of commission. Twenty years ago ... you were giving commissions to people in order to get market or to get product or whatever. Today the legal system has changed. I don't know if it's an improvement or not, I just say it has changed. You can't do it any more. I'm too young in a way to have been in this system, but I agree it was a system.'[5] He admitted that such 'commissions' continued to be paid as late as 2000.

Now Valcke would repay Blatter's loyalty by sorting out the Warner US$10 million problem. On 19 September 2007, as Fifa's secretary-general, he finally did the one thing that those seasoned in the movement of illicit funds would never do – he put pen to paper in a letter from his Zürich office.

Addressed to the Director-General of the Department of Foreign Affairs, Ayanda Ntsaluba, Valcke's letter recorded four neat points under the heading 'Africa Diaspora Legacy Programme'. I was told that Mbeki, Blatter and Fifa official Jérôme Champagne had met to discuss the payment in September, shortly before Valcke was asked to write the letter, but this was not officially confirmed. The points were:

1. The South African Bid and 2010 Fifa World Cup Programme wishes to leave a lasting legacy for football and society.
2. Fifa has launched the 'Win in Africa with Africa' and has committed 70 million USD for the programme.
3. The South African Government has made a commitment of 10 million USD to the legacy programme for the Diaspora and specifically for the Caribbean Countries.
4. We agreed that the fund shall be transferred to the Fifa account in Zürich for Fifa to administer it.

Valcke concluded: 'The account details will be communicated in due course. We thank you for your cooperation.'[6] Valcke's email appeared straightforward: He was reminding the South African government of a commitment, and one of two obvious replies was expected: it would either contest the commitment or it would pay the money.

Instead, what followed was a curious Byzantine silence followed by a complex rerouting of the payment.

Behind the scenes, however, the message of the 'forgotten' payment appears to have made its way to the top.

On 16 November 2007, President Thabo Mbeki addressed an African Union-African Diaspora Ministerial Conference at Gallagher Estate in Midrand, north of Johannesburg.

In the address, he said: 'The African Union fully supported our proposal to Federation of International Football Association (Fifa) that we should treat the 2010 Soccer World Cup which we will host, as an African Soccer World Cup, inclusive of the African Diaspora. Accordingly, therefore, our continent is at one that the 2010 Fifa Soccer World Cup should also benefit the African Diaspora. We remain committed to this goal.'[7]

Whether or not this commitment to the diaspora included the donation of US$10 million remained unsaid.

It was telling that by 7 December 2007 – almost three months later – Valcke had received no reply to his letter to Ntsaluba. If Mbeki was committed to the diaspora programme, his government was strangely mute on the subject.

Valcke wrote a second letter, sending it by email with the September letter attached, this time to South Africa's then Deputy Minister of Finance, Jabu Moleketi.

It was to the point, stating with his trademark grammatical missteps: 'There are few weeks I have sent to you the attached letter. I have never received confirmation but more important I would like to know when the transfer can be done.'

Then Valcke took another step, mentioning that this payment had been discussed by Fifa president Sepp Blatter and South Africa's President Thabo Mbeki: 'This is based on discussion between Fifa and the South African government and also between our President and H.E. President M'Beki.'

He finished off drily: 'Thanks for your feedback.'

The mention of 'discussion' about the US$10 million and Mbeki was a big reality check for the South Africans. It was one thing to brush off a Caribbean shyster, but it was entirely another to brush off Blatter three years before the World Cup was set to be staged.

Something had to be done.

Instead of a response from Moleketi or the Department of Foreign Affairs, Valcke received a prompt reply from none other than the CEO of the South African World Cup Organising Committee, Danny Jordaan.

Three days later, on 10 December 2007, Jordaan addressed him as 'Dear Jerome, Dear Friend'. He explained that there had been a change of plan. It began with a very important reassurance: 'The South African Government has undertaken to pay an amount equivalent to US$10m towards the Fifa World Cup Diaspora Legacy Programme.'

But then Jordaan revealed that he had discussed the matter with Moleketi and the then Foreign Affairs minister, Nkosazana Dlamini-Zuma, 'who has said that the funds should rather be paid over to the 2010 Fifa World Cup Organising Committee South Africa'.

Then he revealed his plan: 'In view of this determination, I want to suggest that Fifa deducts this amount (US$10.0m) from the LOC's [Local Organising Committee's] future operational budget and deals directly with the Diaspora legacy support programme.'[8]

It was all a little confusing. On the one hand, Jordaan suggested the money be 'paid over to' the organising committee, and, on the other, he was suggesting that Fifa 'deducts this amount' from the committee's budget and paid it over to the diaspora programme.

Jordaan ended with 'I trust that Fifa will agree to this arrangement.'

Whether or not Valcke replied to this letter remains unknown, with no parties releasing any further correspondence. Perhaps a reply and further correspondence will emerge should investigators find it in the vast Fifa archive that was seized when the corruption scandal broke in 2015.

What is known is that South Africa's football officials were still not satisfied that their arrangement had been clearly communicated.

Three months after Jordaan's letter, the Safa president, Molefi Oliphant, felt it necessary to further clarify exactly how and to whom the money should be paid.

In a letter to Valcke dated 4 March 2008, Oliphant wrote: 'the South African Football Association requests that Fifa withholds an amount of US$10 million from the Organising Committee's future operational budget funding and thereafter advances the amount withheld to the Diaspora Legacy Programme.'[9]

What was new was that Oliphant – twice in the space of a four-paragraph letter – made it clear that 'The Diaspora Legacy Programme shall be administered and implemented directly by the President of Concacaf who shall act as the fiduciary of the Diaspora Legacy Programme Fund of US$10 million.'[10]

Safa was making it abundantly clear that this money was to go to accounts controlled by Warner.

When the Oliphant letter was made public, in 2015, a strange cross-ing of swords occurred between Oliphant and Jordaan. Oliphant said he was shocked and 'felt betrayed' because Jordaan had not revealed that he had also written to Fifa about the money.[11]

Oliphant said the two had discussed the matter after his letter had become public, but Jordaan had made no mention of the letter he had written. 'I was shocked, disappointed, saddened and felt betrayed because there was no disclosure,' Oliphant told *City Press* newspa-per.[12] Oliphant went further, suggesting that Jordaan had drafted the letter and he had merely signed it in good faith.

'We met twice on Saturday and Sunday discussing this letter [the one I signed] and there was no disclosure from [Jordaan] that a letter was written on December 10 2007. And if you look at both of them, their contents are the same, including the language used, and this sim-ply means they were written by the same person. I signed it because it was given to me by the person I have worked with for more than two decades. It is all about disclosure,' Oliphant said.[13]

He went on to say: 'I can confidently say this letter was drafted by him for me to sign, because the language is the same. I did it in good faith, having confidence and trust in the CEO.'[14]

Oliphant's comments beg the obvious question: if this arrangement was above board and had nothing to do with a bribe, why did he feel 'betrayed' when Jordaan did not disclose that he had also written a let-ter to Fifa? And why did Jordaan not tell him that he had also written to Fifa?

In the space of six months, Valcke's request to the South African government that it honour its commitment to pay Fifa the US$10 million for the diaspora programme had morphed into a convoluted indirect payment involving a deduction from the local organising committee's budget from Fifa.

A second change had occurred. The agreement captured in Valcke's original letter – 'that the fund shall be transferred to the Fifa account in Zürich for Fifa to administer it' – had been abandoned in favour of the money being paid to and directly administered by Jack Warner, who would act as Fifa's 'fiduciary'.

There was another mystery. Why had the payment not been made with the usual fanfare that accompanies such donations? Surely the President or his representative would have handed over the cheque at a public ceremony, making the most of the media attention that such events generate.

And why was the diaspora legacy programme not mentioned at all in the official government website dedicated to the 2010 World Cup? In a section called 'The legacy of the 2010 Fifa World Cup', the site trumpets a series of legacy projects. There is the 'Football turf programme in the host country', the 'Win in Africa with Africa' programme, the 'Football for Hope' programme, the 'Green Goal Programme', the 'My 2010 School Adventure' and the '2010 Fifa World Cup Ticket Fund', among others. But there is no mention at all of a 'Diaspora Legacy Programme'.[15] Was it simply too embarrassing to include this payment because it was dodgy? The diaspora payment was certainly not part of the 'Win in Africa with Africa' programme, the details of which were given with no mention of it at all.

When it came to Fifa's financial report for 2010, the organisation found itself in a bind. It had to account for the US$10 million paid to

Warner, but could not explain this as an indirect payment from South Africa without raising the immediate suspicion that it was a payback of some sort to do with the World Cup.

An inelegant solution was found. In a section with the title 'Development Work', one sentence was tagged on to a lengthy paragraph explaining various payments. It read: 'Since 2008, however, Fifa has also been working on other Win in ... projects that have similar objectives and total funds of USD 53 million: a USD 8 million project has been launched in Oceania, for example, which is aimed at developing national leagues, media coverage, football marketing, futsal and a medical project in the region.

'In South America, another special project, again with a budget of USD 7 million, is focusing on the installation of football turf pitches for each Conmebol member association. Finally, a USD 10 million project has been devised for Concacaf with three objectives: to develop national leagues, to develop youth football and to support the CIES programme of the University of the West Indies (UWI).'

The section makes no mention of this being a payment of the 'diaspora legacy' or that it has anything to do with South Africa. To do so would have been to court the obvious question: was this a bribe?

For now, the secrecy was holding. Disguised and buried as it was deep in a list of other payments that had no connection to South Africa, no questions were asked about it and the payment passed quietly into history until the Fifa scandal broke.

* * *

On 27 May 2015, all hell broke loose when dozens of Swiss law enforcement officials conducted a dawn raid on Zürich's Baur au Lac hotel on the eve of Fifa's 65th Congress, during which Blatter was to stand for re-election as president.

Over 170 years old and boasting views of both the lake and the Alps, a Michelin-starred restaurant and chef and the promise of ultra-exclusivity, 'large marble bathrooms' and 'hardly noticeable technical refinement',[16] the Baur au Lac was the ultimate palace of the rich and pampered and the regular Swiss haunt of the world's football officials travelling to its meetings.

Soon the hotel would provide the backdrop to dramatic video footage showing more than a dozen investigators swooping on the assembled Fifa delegates, arresting some and carrying out boxes of documents and computer hardware for further investigation.

As the grim-looking Fifa delegates were escorted away by police, the FBI released details of the most sensational probe into a world sporting organisation ever conducted. Some 14 officials – nine of them Fifa executives – had been arrested.

In New York, Loretta Lynch, now promoted from the district where she had been behind the Blazer indictment to the position of Attorney General, told a crowded news conference: 'They were expected to uphold the rules that keep soccer honest. Instead they corrupted the business of worldwide soccer to serve their interests and enrich themselves. They did this over and over, year after year, tournament after tournament.'[17]

Swiss authorities, meanwhile, opened their own case against those accused of corrupting the awarding of the 2018 World Cup to Russia and the 2022 World Cup to Qatar. In December 2010, Fifa had taken the unprecedented decision to decide who would host two World Cups at one meeting. It was a classic case of overreach, with multiple opportunities for vote-rigging and vote-trading opening up. Soon enough, there were widespread allegations of bribery. What was particularly galling was that Qatar was not considered a serious football-playing country and its World Cup would likely take place in temperatures in excess of 40 degrees Celsius. It did not take a rocket scientist to figure out that such a decision was not rational.

What was clear was that the governance of football had been shaken to its roots and, for the first time, years of rumoured corruption were likely to be played out in courtrooms.

Five days prior to the swoop, the FBI had filed a 161-page indictment, the outcome of the investigation that had been assisted by Chuck Blazer in Judge Raymond Dearie's courtroom in November 2013.

While the world was staring agog at the Fifa spectacle, South Africa was in shock. The US indictment included a six-page section under the heading '2010 Fifa World Cup Vote Scheme'. This section contained detailed allegations of how bribes had been paid by South African officials to Jack Warner in order to secure three votes in favour of the 2010 World Cup bid.

The bribes were said to have been paid by two people identified as 'Co-Conspirator #15' and 'Co-Conspirator #16'.

The indictment said: 'At various times relevant to the Indictment, Co-Conspirator #15 was a high-ranking official of the 2006 South Africa World Cup bid committee and the 2010 South Africa World Cup bid committee and local organizing committee.' The same language was used to describe 'Co-Conspirator #16'.

There were very few who fitted this description. The South African sports website, Sport24, narrowed it down: 'As best can be determined, only three officials served on both the 2006 World Cup bid committee and the 2010 Soccer World Cup bid committee and local organising committee. They were, Danny Jordaan, Tokyo Sexwale and Irvin Khoza.'[18]

Warner, the indictment said, 'had cultivated ties with South African soccer officials in connection with and subsequent to a failed bid by South Africa to host the 2006 World Cup'.

According to the indictment, Warner's son Daryan – identified as 'Co-Conspirator #14' – had used Warner's 'contacts in South Africa' to organise friendly matches for Concacaf teams in South Africa.

There was one brief paragraph elaborating on an alleged bribe paid to influence Warner to vote for South Africa as the 2006 host. 'At one point, Warner also directed Co-Conspirator #14 to fly to Paris, France and accept a briefcase containing bundles of US currency in US$10000 stacks in a hotel room from Co-Conspirator #15, a high-ranking South African bid committee official. Hours after arriving in Paris, Co-Conspirator #14 boarded a return flight and carried the briefcase back to Trinidad and Tobago, where Co-Conspirator #14 provided it to Warner,'[19] the indictment read.

The indictment then turned to the May 2004 decision to award South Africa the 2010 World Cup.

Warner, it said, had travelled to Morocco where 'a representative of the Moroccan bid committee offered to pay US$1m to Warner in exchange for his agreement to cast his secret ballot on the Fifa executive committee for Morocco to host the 2010 World Cup.'[20]

Then came Chuck Blazer's testimony. Dubbed 'Co-Conspirator #1' in the indictment, he gave his version of what caused the convoluted US$10 million payment to Warner by South Africa.

'Co-Conspirator #1 learned from the defendant Jack Warner that high-ranking officials of Fifa, the South African government, and the South African bid committee, including Co-Conspirator #16, were prepared to arrange for the government of South Africa to pay US$10 million to CFU to "support the African diaspora".'[21]

Then came the crunch: 'Co-Conspirator #1 understood the offer to be in exchange for the agreement of Warner, Co-Conspirator #1, and Co-Conspirator #17 to all vote for South Africa, rather than Morocco, to host the 2010 World Cup.' The unnamed 'Co-Conspirator #17' is described in the indictment as 'a Fifa executive committee member'.

Warner told Blazer he had accepted the offer and would pass on US$1 million to him for his vote for South Africa.

Details of the behind-the-scenes efforts of Blazer and Warner to secure their money emerged on the record for the first time.

After the vote, which took place in 2004, Blazer began to pester Warner for his slice of the money, or, as the formal language of the indictment put it, 'Co-Conspirator #1 periodically asked Warner about the status of the US$10 million payment'.[22]

Warner updated Blazer from time to time, telling him on one occasion that he had learned that the South Africans were unable to pay the money directly from government funds.

'Arrangements were thereafter made with Fifa officials to instead have the US$10 million sent from Fifa – using funds that would otherwise have gone from Fifa to South Africa to support the World

Cup – to CFU.'[23] (It will be recalled that CFU, the Caribbean Football Union, was Warner's organisation.)

This account dovetails with the series of letters described earlier in this chapter in which South African football officials asked Fifa to pay the money out of funds owed to South Africa.

Then a very curious thing happened.

Instead of transferring the US$10 million, a person described as a 'high-ranking Fifa official' made three different payments, of US$616000, US$1600000 and one of US$7784000, which happened to total exactly US$10 million.[24]

This was a very bizarre way to make a payment and it strongly suggested that someone was trying, quite crudely it must be said, to hide the payment in three separate tranches.

It was suspected that Valcke was the 'high-ranking Fifa official', but Fifa suggested it had been another official, the Argentinian Julio H Grondona, a senior vice president and chairman of the finance committee, who had signed off on the payment.[25] Conveniently, Grondona had passed away the year before, in July 2014. The payment was clearly toxic and nobody wanted their fingerprints on it – not even Valcke, who had written to the South Africans to get the money unlocked.

The money was wired from a Fifa account in Switzerland to a Bank of America account in New York 'for credit to accounts held in the names of CFU and Concacaf, but controlled by the defendant Jack Warner, at Republic Bank in Trinidad and Tobago.'[26]

Investigators discovered that soon after receiving these transfers, Warner diverted 'a substantial portion of the funds' for his personal use. One example of this was Warner's instruction to the Republic Bank that US$200 000 of the money be paid into a personal loan account.

The indictment says that Warner laundered some of the money through intermediaries: 'For example, during the period from January 16, 2008 to March 27, 2008, Warner caused approximately US$1.4m of the US$10 million to be transferred to Individual #1, a Trinidadian businessman whose identity is known to the Grand Jury, and Trinidadian Company A, a large supermarket chain in Trinidad and Tobago controlled by Individual #1. Weeks later, checks totaling approximately the same amount and drawn on an account held in the name of Trinidadian Company B, a real estate investment company also controlled by Individual #1, were deposited into a bank account held in the name of Warner and a family member at First Citizens Bank in Trinidad and Tobago.'[27]

The clincher for the bribe allegations is that in the three years after Warner received the US$10 million from Fifa, he made three payments to Blazer that totalled over US$750 000 'in partial payment of the US$1 million that Warner had earlier promised Co-Conspirator #1 as part of the bribe scheme'.[28]

The journey of the Fifa funds through the banking system tells its own story.

Warner's first payment of US$298 500 to Blazer, on 19 December 2008, was made from a CFU account at Republic Bank in Trinidad and Tobago and was made to a Bank of America account in New York 'for credit to an account controlled by Co-Conspirator #1 at a bank in the Cayman Islands'. The second payment was deposited by Blazer into his Merrill Lynch brokerage account in New York.[29]

There was a 'paper trail' – inasmuch as email is the new paper – as, a month earlier, Warner had written to Blazer on 23 August 2010 to advise him that the money was on its way.

The third payment of US$250 000, a cheque, was delivered to Blazer by someone who travelled by plane to JFK International Airport in New York and then went to Blazer's headquarters in Queens to hand it over in person. A representative of the FirstCaribbean International Bank in the Bahamas, where Blazer had another account, then collected the cheque from him and returned to the Bahamas where he deposited it in his account.

Again, Warner had made the amateur mistake of putting things in writing, sending Blazer an email in March 2011 advising him that the third payment was on its way.

The final sentence of the section on South Africa reads: 'Co-Conspirator #1 never received the balance of the promised US$1 million payment.'[30] Could it be that Warner's unwillingness to pay Blazer in full for his 2010 vote added to Blazer's motivation for turning on his 'co-conspirator'?

The US$10 million payment to Jack Warner paints a very uncomfortable picture for South Africa's football and government officials. The facts that are yet to be disproved are as follows:

- The government and football authorities agreed to pay the money to football bodies under Warner's control for the furtherance of the 'diaspora'.
- Warner communicated to Blazer that this amount was 'a bribe' in exchange for his and other votes in favour of South Africa winning the World Cup bid.

- Warner, Blazer and one other voted for South Africa's bid to host the World Cup.

- Warner badgered the South African government to pay over the money.

- The South African government got cold feet and backed out of paying the money.

- A scheme was developed to pay the money out of Fifa money owed to South Africa.

- South African football authorities made it plain in writing that the funds were to be under the personal administration of Warner.

- The money was transferred to Warner-controlled bank accounts in three separate tranches for reasons that have not been explained.

- Much of the money was then laundered by Warner and used for personal purposes.

- Blazer was paid US$750000 by Warner, which he clearly understood to be a bribe payment for his vote in favour of South Africa hosting the 2010 tournament.

In addition to this, two of Mbeki's cabinet ministers, Mosiuoa Lekota and Ronnie Kasrils – both of whom have since fallen out with the ANC leadership – have publicly stated that there was never any discussion about a US$10 million payment to Caribbean football.

Lekota said: 'Never once was anything like this discussed in that cabinet. We didn't know anything. If this was an honest thing, why didn't they tell South Africa? There is no way we can say this was authorised by government. It is nothing else but a cover-up for a bribe that was indeed a bribe.'[31] Kasrils said he had 'no recollection of that (subject) ever being discussed or such a decision being taken while (he) was in cabinet'.[32]

South Africa's football officials and the government have maintained that the legacy payment was a legitimate, above-board fulfilment of a 2010 World Cup commitment.

In March 2016, the 'legacy' defence was dealt another blow when Fifa stated for the first time that it believed South Africa had paid a bribe. In a 22-page 'Victim Statement and Request for Restitution' filed with a US court, Fifa said Warner had 'strong illicit ties to the South African bid committee'.[33] The legal document said Morocco had offered Warner a bribe, but 'the South Africans offered a more attractive bribe of US$10m in exchange for Warner's, Blazer's and a third Executive Committee member's votes'.[34] Warner and South African officials had 'lied to Fifa about the nature of the payment, disguising it as support for the benefit of the "African Diaspora" in the Caribbean region, when in reality it was a bribe'.[35]

After the South African government reacted with anger to the bribe claim, Fifa issued a statement to explain what it meant: 'The US indictments do not allege that South Africa "bought" the World Cup with bribes. Nor does FIFA. The US indictments, which FIFA is relying upon in its restitution request, merely accuses certain individuals of criminal behaviour." What was meant by 'criminal behaviour' was not clarified.[36]

While the government and football officials were figuring out how to get the money paid to Warner, the stadiums continued to rise around the country. But, behind the scenes, an entirely different species of graft was evolving as company directors met in secret to decide how to skim as much money as possible from the construction tenders.

CHAPTER 5

What a carve-up

'It's incredible that with the scale of collusion that we are looking at in this hearing, everyone can come and say, "I didn't know".'

– Yasmin Carrim

From the top of Signal Hill, part of Cape Town's Table Mountain complex, the view is magnificent. In the distance is Robben Island, where Nelson Mandela spent decades in jail. The choppy waters of Table Bay lap against the docks of the Victoria & Alfred Waterfront – the city's premier tourist destination, with its repurposed warehouses offering upmarket shopping and accommodation.

Cape Town's City Bowl curls up in an arc to the right, running up the slopes of Table Mountain before giving way to a protected reserve.

And, in the foreground, on a green strip of parkland, stands a magnificent stadium, its roof a sweeping white disc. At night, when the lights come on, the structure's translucent skin glows white.

While it is pleasant to look at, Cape Town Stadium is a financial black hole. It had its moment during the 2010 World Cup, but that moment passed and it is now a massive, budget-sapping white elephant that will be funded by generations of taxpayers.

The tale of how this architectural fantasy became reality is a sobering one, in which a toxic mixture of corporate greed, institutional arrogance and government weakness opened the way for one of the single biggest moments of wasteful expenditure in post-apartheid South Africa.

In South Africa's 2010 bid book, the local organising committee (LOC) had been modest to a fault, proposing that the old rugby stadiums of Ellis Park in Johannesburg, King's Park in Durban and Newlands in Cape Town be used as venues, alongside a refurbished Soccer City, which would be enclosed.

The country was still in the thrall of then president Thabo Mbeki's 'fiscal discipline' regime. The approach was simple: capital expenditure was to be carefully weighed up against what it would achieve to develop those communities that had been neglected under apartheid or to grow the economy. The watchword was 'sustainability'.

The bid committee's proposal that the old rugby stadiums be used, with some modest upgrades, struck the right note under this policy.

But once the bid had been accepted, a rising tide of national fervour over the hosting of the tournament opened the door for the construction project to mushroom into a public spending spree the likes of which the country had not seen since the 1999 arms deal became mired in allegations of corruption.

By the time the tournament kicked off, both King's Park and Newlands had been dumped as venues. Instead, a proposal to build Cape Town's shimmering stadium and another brand-new stadium in Durban, as well as several other major upgrades or new stadiums elsewhere, had been accepted.

69

The absurdity of the decision is painfully obvious. The original bid had made much of the proximity of King's Park to Durban International Airport, located a short drive from the city centre. By the time the project planners and their hangers-on had finished spending, the airport would be shut down and replaced by a totally new airport some 40 km from the city.

The new airport, at La Mercy, would not lead to any improvement in the servicing of air travel to and from Durban. Inexplicably, like the old airport, it too had only one runway. This was spending for spending's sake, and it would be cruelly exposed during the World Cup, when the brand-new airport could not cope with the dozens of private jets flying VIPs in to watch the semifinal. With not a little irony, the old airport had to be temporarily opened to accommodate the extra traffic.

The potential for 'mega-projects', such as the construction of stadiums and airports, to attract careless expenditure or, worse, outright crookery, was overlooked as the government threw the fiscal rulebook out the window and backed the massive spending programme.

In 2004, the auditing firm Grant Thornton had estimated that the taxpayer would pay R2.3 billion towards the provision of stadiums and infrastructure. This had increased to R8.35 billion by October 2006.[1] Government would eventually blow more than R11 billion on the stadium project.

In his budget review in February 2010, then Finance minister Pravin Gordhan told Parliament, 'The Fifa World Cup is expected to contribute about 0.5% of GDP growth in 2010.' But this number had a sting in its tail. Totalling up all expenditure on the tournament, he added,

'To date, government has spent about R33 billion in preparation for the tournament.'[2]

More than 10 per cent of this money – some R4.5 billion – was spent on the construction of Cape Town Stadium in the Green Point precinct alone.

Newlands first lost ground as the stadium of choice when the Cape Town City Council – then under the control of the ANC – decided that Athlone Stadium, on the Cape Flats, would be a better option. Their reasoning was simple: renovating the stadium, situated in a relatively poor area, would bring much-needed development. And, they reasoned, the Cape Flats was where the city's football fans lived.

It seemed, on the face of it, a 'no-brainer'. Development money would go where it was needed and the stadium would continue to be the home of local football after the World Cup, ensuring it would be regularly used. It was a long shot, but there was the possibility that the gate takings from local games would relieve the city of the burden of fully funding the renovations.

The province's then premier, Ebrahim Rasool, supported the city's choice of Athlone Stadium, stating that 'the province and the city of Cape Town have always felt that the development of a dedicated football stadium in Athlone will leave a lasting legacy for generations to come. In addition, the building of the stadium will allow us to leverage much-needed transport and other socio-economic developments in the surrounding area.'[3]

But this was not to be. In November 2005, Fifa president Sepp Blatter breezed into town. By the time he left, Newlands and Athlone had been dumped in favour of a new stadium. Investigative writers

Karen Schoonbee and Stefaans Brümmer explained how it all happened, in an article entitled 'Public loss, Fifa's gain'.[4]

Blatter met with Ebrahim Rasool at the luxury Arabella Sheraton Hotel. He talked of the city's 'spectacular scenery' and made the ANC politician a tantalising offer: in addition to group fixtures, the city could be the host of one of the tournament's quarterfinal and semifinal games. The massive global television audience and the prestige attached to such an event would be second only to the hosting of the final, which it had already been decided would take place at Soccer City, near Soweto.

There was one small problem. The hosting of a semifinal required a larger stadium – one capable of seating in excess of 60 000 spectators. The renovation of Newlands and Athlone would both fall short of this number.

Later that day Blatter took the matter further in a meeting with Mbeki. The Fifa boss was treated like a visiting head of state from a major nation and could summon anyone he wished, from the President down, to a meeting whenever he felt like it.

Subsequent to Blatter's meeting with Mbeki, the idea of a new stadium for Cape Town took on new momentum. Whatever 'fiscal discipline' had been exercised when drawing up the bid documents was now well and truly gone. In its place was a plan to spend – and spend big – on stadiums and related infrastructure.

Mbeki's closest aide, Essop Pahad, who held the title of Minister in the Presidency, called Rasool and said that Cape Town needed to build the new stadium at Green Point.[5]

Blatter had spoken, and although his preference for a new stadium was couched in polite language, his decision was final. The regulations governing the hosting of the World Cup clearly stated: 'The organising association is subject to the supervision and control of Fifa, which has the last word on all matters relevant to the 2010 Fifa World Cup. The decisions of Fifa are final.'[6]

A series of bureaucratic encounters between the city and national government were to follow, with the decision being hammered down with ever-greater authority from above. Eventually, the city's mayor, Nomaindia Mfeketo – a member of the ruling ANC – could resist no more, and on 16 February she signed off on Green Point as the Cape Town venue.

Blatter put his signature on the document on 15 March – one day ahead of schedule. There may have been a reason for his haste. The next day, on 16 March, a new coalition formed in the Cape Town City Council and Mfeketo was deposed in favour of opposition leader Helen Zille, a virulent critic of the building of the new stadium.

Later that month, Zille ordered a halt to contracting for the stadium and commissioned two consultancies to compare Green Point with five other venues.

The results of this report, compiled by Zunaid Moolla, were devastating for Green Point. The original cost estimation of R1.28 billion was replaced with a new estimate: R3.08 billion, making it easily the most expensive option. Green Point's revenue-earning potential was the second worst of the options and it scored lowest on its contribution to development.

But Green Point was the only proposal with the seating to accommodate a semifinal. As Zille put it: 'The provincial and national governments have said that we must host a semi-final or we lose 2010. This is the choice that we face as a council.'[7]

In any event, Zille's objections were moot as her predecessor had signed off on the plan before being booted out of office.

Once the council had been battered into submission, Blatter's vision of a showpiece stadium, a jewel in the World Cup crown, was adopted along with its financial consequences. The modest upgrade of Newlands had morphed into a no-expenses-spared flight of design fancy.

The city's 2010 website breathlessly described the stadium with these words: 'Enwrapped by a façade of woven fibreglass, coated with Teflon, it will resemble a rose-coloured bowl floating on a base, when lit up at night. The architects have dubbed the stadium "the Diva of Cape Town", reflecting the constantly changing moods of the city in varying weather conditions.

'The design and construction of the roof is unique throughout the world. Its basic structure resembles a bicycle wheel, open in the middle. Some 72 cables linking the outer and inner rings of the circle were slowly tightened to raise the roof from ground level to its present height. Another first for the roof is the use of 16 mm thick panels of glass to cover and protect the spectators from strong winds and rain. This will let in the light while the ceiling panels underneath – made of woven PVC fabric – will soften the noise from within.'[8]

According to an article in *Civil Engineering*, 'The 37 000 m^2 hanging steel and glass roof is the largest of its kind in the world.'

All of these cutting-edge design features and materials did not come cheap. Between December 2006, when tenders closed, and December

2009, the stadium would be built from the ground up. The main contractors were two of South Africa's leading construction firms, Murray & Roberts and WBHO, who were asked by the city to merge their bids. By the time they finished building, the cost of the project would have ballooned to an incredible R4.5 billion.

And it wasn't just in Cape Town that the spending spun out of control. In the much poorer Nelson Mandela Bay metro of the Eastern Cape, more than R2 billion was spent on a new 45 000-seater stadium. The stadium was initially costed at R1.7 billion, leading to a budget shortfall of R300 million, which became the responsibility of the cash-strapped municipality.

The then city manager, Graham Richards, said the building of the stadium 'will impact adversely on our ability to spend on infrastructure over the next 15 years. My view is that unless national government finds a way to mitigate this effect it will definitely impact negatively and my other colleagues agree.'[9]

In Durban, the original proposal in the bid document to revamp the King's Park rugby stadium, at a cost of R54 million, for use during the World Cup was shelved in favour of the construction of the brand-new Moses Mabhida Stadium.

The story of how the modest upgrade of an existing stadium morphed into a mega-project aimed at creating a sporting precinct and a brand-new stadium has strong parallels with what occurred in Cape Town. But while the Cape Town metro council had resisted national and provincial government's insistence on a big stadium build, here the local authority, province and the national government were all on the same page.

In early 2005, the local authority and the KwaZulu-Natal provincial government adopted a '2010 and Beyond' strategy, which had lofty ambitions, including, for the first time, mention of 'a new soccer stadium'. Durban's then mayor, Obed Mhlaba, began talking of the need for a 'specialist soccer stadium' because, he said, 'Durban needs a new home for soccer'.[10]

In his 'City Manager's Newsletter', the then city manager, Mike Sutcliffe, said: 'The Bid Book had indicated that ABSA Stadium [King's Park] would be upgraded but when the costs of that upgrading escalated to over ten times what was indicated in the bid book we started exploring alternative options. After reporting to the Premier and Mayor and after the Premier made a submission to the national Inter-Ministerial Committee, it was accepted that we should build an iconic stadium. This strategy has been endorsed by EXCO and Council.'[11]

What had started out as a fiscally conservative upgrade of an existing stadium had grown wings to become an ambitious plan to turn Durban into a global sporting hub.

'Not only do we have favourable regional climatic conditions and excellent infrastructure, but we have the potential to host the 42 main Olympic sporting codes in the King's Park Precinct. We are certainly well placed to become Africa's best sporting, leisure, arts and culture destination. When combined with our rich cultural, historical and political legacy we have all the ingredients for our "2010 and Beyond" strategy to place us at the forefront of sport, art and heritage,'[12] said Sutcliffe.

What was needed was an 'iconic' stadium that would be part of a complex that would enable Durban to bid for future Commonwealth and Olympic Games hosting rights.

The '2010 and Beyond' document now talked of a choice having to be made between upgrading King's Park and erecting a new stadium. It listed three points in favour of the upgrade and 12 against it. The document concluded: 'The province and the city have decided to opt for a new stadium on the site of the existing King's Park Soccer Stadium.'[13]

The CEO of Sharks Rugby, Brian van Zyl, soon received a letter from the 2010 organising committee CEO, Danny Jordaan, informing him that the rugby stadium would not be a venue.

Soon the stadium tender process was rolling, with a very serious commitment being made not to exceed a R1.6 billion budget limit.

But there were ambitious plans that soon put paid to fiscal discipline. By the time it was completed, it was clear that a combination of aesthetic overreach and fiscal indiscipline had produced another construction colossus of questionable sustainability. The most financially solvent potential rental client, Sharks Rugby, was clearly not going to sign up.

The central feature of the 70 000-seater stadium was a soaring 106-m arch reaching over the pitch. The stadium construction bill included a cable car designed to take visitors up to the highest point of the arch.

The final bill for the stadium was an eye-watering R3.1 billion.

Even the showpiece Soccer City stadium – host to the opening game and the final – was not exempt from controversy. The stadium was built at a cost of R3.4 billion and could seat up to 94 000, although fewer seats were available during the World Cup. Here a different species of financial irregularity was scurrying about.

Investigative journalist Rob Rose discovered that the empowerment credentials of an outfit called 'National Stadium SA' (NSSA), which had been awarded a ten-year contract to manage Soccer City, were suspect. NSSA was 50 per cent owned by Global Event Management (GEM).

According to South African law, companies are required to have black economic empowerment (BEE) credentials before they are awarded government contracts. Empowerment is an attempt to address the ownership and control of business, which was skewed in favour of the white minority by decades of racist lawmaking. But, instead of including genuine black businessmen, some companies game the system by placing the names of lowly employees on their letterheads to pretend that they are up with the legal requirements.

According to Rose, there were serious questions about GEM's 'empowerment partner', Gladwin Khangale. 'The first factor to arouse suspicions is that the 42-year-old Khangale was appointed as a director of GEM only on 1 October 2007 – a few months before the invitation to tender was announced,' wrote Rose.[14]

Also odd was that 'a breakdown of responsibilities, filed with the tender documents, records that while Khangale owns 26 per cent of the company and supposedly spends 100 per cent of his time at GEM, he has no financial responsibility for signing of loans, cheques, surety, acquisitions or any major contracts. Nor does he have the power to hire or fire anyone.'[15]

Rose tracked down Khangale's home address and found it was in a low-income area west of the small town of Heidelberg. He approached Khangale to get his side of the story. 'He was jittery and said "I don't think

I can disclose anything." He confirmed that he owned the shares at one stage, but said he no longer owned them. But when asked what happened that led to him disposing of the shares, Khangale clammed up, saying "I can't explain that to you … there's some confidentiality on that."'

GEM managing director and NSSA director Hank Ferreira simply contradicted Khangale's claim to have relinquished the shares, saying Khangale 'is still a shareholder … The shares are still issued. Nothing has changed per our tender bid.'[16]

Rose dug further and discovered that, before his elevation to major shareholder, Khangale had been a security guard in 2001. According to Ferreira, he was 'pulled through the ranks and put through our in-house training'.[17]

Ferreira said: 'I get frustrated when people refer to so-called window dressing, and I invite anyone to come and investigate the minute book because there's a path of issuing the shares.'[18]

Rose uncovered several other oddities, including one man's story of how he lost out on a tender because he would not pay a bribe. Vivian Lottering, the CEO of Great African Seating, was asked to submit a tender for seating at the stadium. 'We were very confident because it was pretty much our product specified in the tender request. We did an excellent presentation to the adjudicators and our product and price was very competitive,'[19] he told Rose.

But Lottering soon hit a brick wall. He says he was contacted by one of the officials and told: 'The job is yours, but my hand is heavy.'[20] Asked what it would take to move his heavy hand, the official told him that R2 million should do it. Lottering said he could not afford to pay a bribe.

Rose describes how, the following Monday, Lottering's Great African Seating got a letter saying that its bid had been turned down: 'Lottering says he was bitter, and approached various members of Safa and other forums without luck.'[21]

But this was petty crime compared to the grand scheme cooked up by big business to cash in on the stadium contracts.

* * *

The escalation in the cost of building new stadiums was not just a function of Fifa's pressure to produce 'jewels' for its World Cup event. It would later be revealed that construction companies had colluded on bidding and had rigged the prices of the stadiums. The Competition Commission of South Africa investigated what came to be known as the 'construction cartel', consisting of at least 15 construction companies.

The 15 companies would eventually reach a settlement in which they admitted to 'collusive tendering' in a string of projects, including the construction of World Cup stadiums. The story of the collusion by the construction companies would make a fine script for a Martin Scorsese movie.

In an affidavit submitted to the Competition Tribunal, an investigator in the Competition Commission's Cartel Division, Fhatuwani Mudimeli, described how South Africa's big construction firms rigged the tenders.

It all began rather innocently. In July 2006, after South Africa won the right to host the 2010 World Cup, the local organising committee convened a meeting of construction firms and other industry 'stakeholders' at the Sandton Sun Hotel in Johannesburg 'to discuss the construction of stadia for the 2010 Fifa World Cup'.[22]

Keen to get in on the action, all the big firms sent representatives. Present were senior employees of construction firms WBHO, Murray & Roberts, Group Five, Stefanutti Stocks and Aveng.

The organising committee described the purpose of the meeting as 'to hold discussions regarding the delivery and development of [stadia and other facilities] for 2010'.[23] The committee went on to say: 'The major industry players need to inform the LOC about the current activity in Rand value terms and geographic spread in the country and relate this to the skills capacity to take up additional projects of international importance.'[24]

The menu was appetising. The committee told the firms it wanted to build four new stadiums, perform major upgrades to two more, a 'medium upgrade' to another and minor upgrades at three others. That made ten stadium-build projects.

The firms were informed that a formal tender document would be issued in August 2006 and the committee expected responses to be filed by the end of November 2006. Because of the urgency of the build programme, they were told that 'existing structures for the delivery of the projects – such as standard tendering processes – would not be capable of meeting the timing requirements, and that other modes of procurement were to be considered'.

Once it was apparent that big money was on offer, the construction firms decided to do whatever it took to get the job done with as nice a profit margin as possible. In terms of South Africa's competition law, it is illegal for competitors to share information or to in any way collude over tenders. But this is exactly what South Africa's top firms would do.

In September, representatives of the construction firms met at the offices of WBHO in Sandton, the corporate capital of South Africa, where the building firms had put up one gleaming skyscraper after another as business fled the 'crime and grime' of the Johannesburg city centre. Present were: Mike Wylie, the CEO of WBHO; Louwtjie Nel, the MD of the firm's building division; Phillip Taylor, the senior estimator of Murray & Roberts; Schalk Ackerman, the MD of Aveng's Civils Division; Trevor Robinson, the MD of Concor's Civils Division; Mike Lomas, the CEO of Group Five; and Kobus von Biljon, the CEO of Basil Read.

It was like a meeting of Mafia dons in the back room of a Chicago pasta joint. They didn't just share information. At the meeting they discussed exactly how the tenders for the stadiums would be carved up between them.

They met again on 6 October 2006. The same people were present, with the exception of Nel. At the second meeting, also at WBHO's Sandton offices, they discussed 'the allocation of the projects to build the various stadia among the construction firms'. They talked about 'which construction firms would submit tenders, or which construction firms were interested in submitting tenders'.[25]

Rigging tenders for so many projects in so many different locations is hard work. It wasn't simply a matter of deciding who would get what. They also had to agree on who would submit 'cover prices' for the tenders. The 'cover price', said Mudimeli, was 'a price that was submitted by a supplier for a tender that was not intended to win the tender'.[26] The bid in which a 'cover price' was used was called a 'cover bid'.

The crafting of a cover price was essential to ensure that the bidding appeared competitive while one of the bids was advantaged over the others. There were many ways to skin this cat. You could simply bid too high. Or you could be more subtle and submit conditions that you knew would be unacceptable to the client.

In order for a cover price to succeed, the company submitting it had to collude with the company submitting the 'winning' tender and with others who would stay out of the bidding altogether.

The meeting then turned to those who were not present – companies that could 'upset the system proposed at the meeting'.[27] And there was the matter of who would partner with whom to help deliver the big projects where one company couldn't do it all on its own.

The details were worked out. It was agreed that before submitting a tender, the companies would review the proposed bids and cover bids 'to establish that, in each instance, the cover bid was less competitive than the allocated tenderer's bid, and that the tender price of each bid was lower than the cover prices'.[28]

Then began the big carve-up. The tender for Durban's Moses Mabhida Stadium – named after a communist stalwart of the anti-apartheid struggle – would go to WBHO. They would partner with Group Five, and Grinaker would submit a cover bid.

The massive refurbishment tender for Soccer City, near Johannesburg and Soweto, would go to Grinaker, with Covac submitting a cover bid.

Cape Town's Green Point Stadium (as it was then called) would go to Murray & Roberts in a joint venture with WBHO.

Nelspruit's Mbombela Stadium would be allocated to Concor and

Hochtief in a join venture, with Group Five and Basil Read/Bouygues submitting cover bids.

Polokwane's Peter Mokaba Stadium would go to Stefanutti Stocks, with Concor, WBHO or Group Five submitting cover bids.

Nelson Mandela Bay Stadium would go to Stefanutti Stocks.

Not content to divide up the cake, the firms also agreed on a profit margin of 17.5 per cent on all these projects.

It worked like clockwork. The plan was implemented with great efficiency. In the case of Green Point Stadium, the lowest bid came from a WBHO and Murray & Roberts joint venture. To the delight of the bidders and their partners in crime, it won. The City of Cape Town, oblivious to the collusion, was doing the right thing and going for the least expensive option.

In Johannesburg, Grinaker won, and in Durban, WBHO won as planned.

When they were caught out four years after the World Cup had come and gone, the construction firms agreed to pay R1.5 billion – R1 463 814 392 to be exact – in penalties. The two biggest amounts were paid by Murray & Roberts (R309 million) and WBHO (R311 million) – the two main contractors for the Cape Town Stadium.[29]

With this payment, the construction firms settled no fewer than 90 contraventions of the Competitions Act.

But they first had to appear before the Competition Tribunal, the adjudicative arm of the Competition Commission.

The *City Press* newspaper reported: 'Many of the senior construction executives present spoke about wanting to put this "dark chapter" behind them. Under cross-examination from the tribunal panel, however, they admitted that many still had implicated executives and managers in their employ – and that some of these employees were still involved in administering tenders for the companies.'[30]

Two frustrated members of the tribunal panel, Norman Manoim and Yasmin Carrim, tried to get the 'guilty cartel members to explain how the collusion had happened and what the rationale behind these decisions was'.[31] Carrim said it seemed they had come to the tribunal with 'copy and paste' answers, and someone joked that it appeared they had even colluded on their responses. 'It's incredible that with the scale of collusion that we are looking at in this hearing, everyone can come and say "I didn't know", said Carrim.'[32]

Pressed on why an implicated employee was still on the payroll, one of the construction bosses – Neil Cloete, CEO of G Liviero & Son – said: 'We have taken the view that cover prices were endemic in the industry. In our view the individual did not act outside the inherent behaviour of the industry.'[33] That a company could seriously attempt to justify illegal behaviour by claiming that this was how it was done 'in the industry' demonstrated a complete ethical failure.

Murray & Roberts CEO, Henry Laas, told the tribunal that the finding of collusion was 'the bleakest moment' in his company's history.[34] He quoted Nelson Mandela: 'If there are dreams about a beautiful South Africa, there are also roads that lead to their goal. Two of these roads could be named Goodness and Forgiveness.'[35]

The CEO of Raubex, Rudolf Fourie, said the World Cup was to blame for the collusion. 'It was not only stadiums that were built in this country. There were substantial road networks upgraded too.'[36]

Laas went further after the commission hearing and penned an apology to the nation, which was carried in South Africa's largest business newspaper, claiming that his company, Murray & Roberts, was 'woven into the very fabric of South Africa and we are fiercely proud of our heritage'.

'I know that the Competition Commission's findings of collusion in the construction sector has angered and disappointed you, just as it has our board, executives, employees, shareholders and other stakeholders.

'And for that, on behalf of Murray & Roberts, I have one fundamental response. An unequivocal apology.'[37]

How 'unequivocal' the apology was immediately came into question when Laas claimed, a few paragraphs later, that, 'This collusive conduct was never known to, and much less endorsed, by our board. It was the result of unauthorised actions of a handful of directors in our subsidiary companies.'

And, he said later on, 'Companies don't commit offences, but people do.'[38]

Laas complained that the penalty imposed by the tribunal was too severe. 'We accept that Murray & Roberts should be penalised for its historical collusive conduct, but not to the extent that it will significantly handicap our ability to contribute towards future infrastructural development. The past three years have been a very challenging financial period for the group and the R309m fine is a severe penalty that will serve as a stark reminder of this conduct that must never be repeated.'[39]

The grand visions of Fifa and the less grand schemes of the construction companies saddled government at all three levels with a massive capital spending bill.

But that was not all. Once the Fifa train left town after the semifinal, the City of Cape Town found itself with a very expensive white elephant.

In 2012, Mayor Patricia de Lille became the latest city leader to be saddled with the stadium's mounting costs. The council oversaw a new report, 'Business Plan for Cape Town Stadium and Green Point Park', which lamented: 'Following the event, the stadium is proving to be costly to the City of Cape Town and its citizens, as a result of being used less than it could. The reasons are many, not least the prolonged economic recession, the failure to attract a premium anchor tenant, and extremely restrictive zoning laws that apply to the land on which the stadium and park are built.'[40]

The stadium has hosted a number of concerts as well as the occasional sporting event. Over two days in December 2015, it was the venue for the South African leg of the World Rugby Sevens Series tour. In this particular case, Cape Town's gain came at Port Elizabeth's expense. The event had been hosted at Nelson Mandela Bay Stadium – another World Cup structure with little prospect of breaking even.

The citizens of Cape Town – and those of other cities with similar white elephants – will be paying for the World Cup for decades to come. It turned out that the beautiful concrete visions of architectural splendour that had hosted the 2010 World Cup literally had rotten foundations. Once the construction firms had finished and the stadiums hosted their first games for the national team, yet another species of graft would crawl out of the shadows to take a slice of the beautiful game. In Singapore, a match-fixer was planning a trip to South Africa to cash in on the Bafana Bafana warm-up games.

CHAPTER 6

The fix is in

'Chaibou walked into a bank in a small South African city carrying
a bag filled with as much as US$100 000 in $100 bills, according
to another referee travelling with him. The deposit was so large that
a bank employee gave Mr Chaibou a gift of commemorative coins
bearing the likeness of Nelson Mandela.'

– Report in *The New York Times*

One evening in May 2010, Bafana Bafana played Guatemala at the
Peter Mokaba Stadium in Polokwane, capital of Limpopo province. It
was an extraordinary game.

Referee Ibrahim Chaibou of Niger had a busy night. So busy that he
appeared to be losing his focus. He awarded two handball penalties,
though it was plain to all that, in both cases, the ball never came near
the hand of the accused player.

A stunning last-minute strike by Bernard Parker put the icing on a
fantastic 5–0 victory that signalled that Bafana's World Cup prepara-
tions had paid off.

By this time, World Cup fever had gripped the country. Fans were
encouraged to wear their Bafana shirts on Fridays and the yellow strip

was proudly on display everywhere. Car mirrors were covered in gloves bearing the national colours and flags fluttered from car windows as the nation got behind the team.

The fact that Bafana were winning on the field added to the hype. The team's excellent performance in the Guatemala friendly and in four other games – against Thailand, Colombia, Bulgaria and Denmark – was the subject of some pride.

But Chaibou's poor performance during the Guatemala game was no fluke. Two years later the country would learn with shock that Chaibou was blowing his whistle to please a global betting syndicate that had managed to take over the refereeing of Bafana games ahead of the World Cup.

It all began in early 2010 when a man identifying himself as 'Mohamed' appeared at the South African Football Association's (Safa) headquarters on the Soccer City precinct outside Soweto.

He was carrying a letter bearing the masthead of an organisation called 'Football4U Int'l'. It gave its address as 'Blk 640, 601-58 Rowell Road, Singapore'.

Dated 29 April 2010, the letter was addressed to 'Mr Nematandani Kirsten'. The name and surname had been mixed up; it was in fact addressed to Kirsten Nematandani, the then president of Safa.

The letter, which was copied to Safa's chief operating office (COO), Dennis Mumble, and the head of national teams, Lindile 'Ace' Kika, was headed: 'RE: REFEREES EXCHANGE PROGRAM'. It referred to an earlier 'meeting on the above mentioned matter in Johannesburg' before going on to say: 'We are extremely keen to work closely with your good office on the referees exchange program as discussed. We will be inviting

South African Fifa qualified match officials for international friendly matches and league matches in Middle East countries whereby we act as agents for the supply of referees and assistant referees.

'And in return we will be pleased to assist SAFA in providing Fifa qualified referees and assistant referees from CAF to officiate warm up international friendly in South Africa from May 2010 to June 2010.'[1]

The man called Mohamed – later identified by Fifa as betting syndicate member Jason Jo Lourdes – met with officials and a deal was struck. To the cash-strapped national football association, the arrangement was manna from heaven. Football4U was offering to provide Fifa-accredited referees, covering their expenses, travel costs and accommodation at its own expense. And it was offering to pay for the use of South African referees in international tournaments.

But there were several obvious flaws to the offer that would have been picked up by an alert official. For one thing, Football4U gave its email address as 'foot_ball4u@yahoo.com.sg'. It is highly unusual for a credible business to use a free Yahoo email address to conduct official business. The second was that Wilson Raj Perumal, a man with links to the betting underworld, signed the letter. If they had bothered to investigate him or his organisation, they would have discovered that he had been exposed for trying to fix a match in China eight months earlier.[2]

Perumal, who was jailed in 2011, when the law finally caught up with him in Finland, would claim to have fixed 'around 80–100 football matches' across the world, pocketing some US$5 million, all of which, he says, he lost to gambling.[3]

He told the cable network CNN: 'I was on the bench at times, and telling players what to do, giving orders to the coach. It was that easy. There was no policing whatsoever.'[4]

Perumal spelled out his methods in an extraordinary self-published autobiography with the title *Kelong Kings: Confessions of the World's Most Prolific Match-Fixer*. The book, which reveals how he built a global match-fixing racket, includes details of how he fixed the Bafana games. Perumal lays out his modus operandi in great detail in chapters explaining how he fixed earlier games involving the Zimbabwean national team during a tournament in Malaysia.

'Language is very important: things must be told in the right way so that when you put everything on the table, people don't back away. "OK, that's 50-50-50, three matches, $150 000", I ran the presentation over in my head. "Then if we decide that you proceed to the next round of the tournament, it's another 50 thousand. In total you'll be making around $200 000", I paused. That's a lot of money.'[5]

Perumal worked on his voice, believing that it was all-important to sound right when you dangled the carrot of corruption before an official. 'In order to convince someone you've got a plan, you've got to speak like Robert de Niro. He is one of my favourite actors, as is Morgan Freeman; I like listening to them speak. It's not easy to sound like them; if only I were blessed with the way these guys talk, things would be much simpler. In my next life, I wish to have Morgan Freeman's voice.'[6]

The penurious Zimbabwean football fraternity made easy pickings for Perumal and his Morgan Freeman drawl. 'Deep inside, I knew that the Zimbabweans needed money; one hundred US dollars in Zimbabwe was a lot of money, and here we were talking about hundreds of thousands of dollars. According to my calculation, I had an 80 percent success rate; I had already fixed with Zimbabwe in 1997 [and] knew how vulnerable they were, I could almost read their minds.'[7]

He had the shallowest interest in the countries he visited, thinking only of how he might make a fast buck by corrupting their football authorities. In Zimbabwe, his disdain was immense. 'As we drove from the airport to town, I thought: Fuck this country is backdated.'[8]

Perumal's shtick was simple. He found an official, gave them the flimsiest of identifications and then, after chatting for a while, put the money on the table: 'I showed up at the Zimbabwe FA's offices with only a name-card in my pocket ... I'm not a formal person and I don't like wearing ties, but I was nonetheless decently attired. I met the Zimbabwean official who introduced himself as Jumbojumbo.'[9]

Once introduced, Perumal said he was aware of Zimbabwe's 'quite bad' economic situation. He was offering something for free: an all-expenses-paid trip to Malaysia to participate in an eight-team tournament with a group stage, quarterfinals, semis and a final. 'There's no prize money up for grabs and we will not pay you an appearance fee but we will give you 30 tickets to fly to Malaysia and have a good time.'

'Then I added, "If you want to make extra money, I also have another idea. You see, as the promoter of the tournament, it is my duty to bring the host team to the final. Some teams will have to make way for the Malaysian team. We have a capacity crowd, so Malaysia has to make it all the way. If you give me your cooperation, if the whole team cooperates, I will give you fifty thousand dollars per match."'

Perumal sat back and allowed the offer to sink in before adding, in his best De Niro voice, that 'the coach, the players, everybody needs to dance to our tune. We will pay you cash on completion of each job, 50 thousand dollars after each game, 50-50-50, three matches, 150 thousand dollars. Then, if we decide that you will quality for the semi-finals, it's another 50. In total, you'll be making about 200 thousand dollars."'

Another pause before adding: 'That's a lot of money.'

And then came the clincher: 'Everything is paid for: tickets, accommodation, extras ... and here is ten thousand dollars for you. Take it as a gift on my part. I don't know if you will be able to convince your superiors. If you won't be able to, then just keep these ten thousand. But if you will, then there will be 200 thousand dollars waiting for you out there in Malaysia.'

The next day, when he called Jumbojumbo he got the response: 'We are ready. No problem.'[10]

Once in Malaysia, Perumal's helper Thana got to work. 'Thana's guys were all over the players, buying them mobile phones, football boots, jerseys, shorts and other gifts. The players were like children walking into a candy store; Thana really put them on a shopping spree.

'"Take what you want", he kept repeating with a smile, "but just give us the result."'[11]

Before the first match, Perumal made his point again: '"Listen", I told the Zimbabwean players before their first match in the cup, "this game has got no value: It's not a World Cup qualifier; it's not an Olympic qualifier; nobody is going to remember you for winning this match or this tournament. Win or lose, you are not going to go anywhere. But if you do as I say there are 40 thousand dollars for you players to share."'[12]

Perumal also fixed a string of matches featuring Zimbabwe in what came to be known as the 'Asiagate scandal' between 2007 and 2009.[13] No fewer than 93 players and officials were suspended, for periods ranging from six months to lifetime bans.[14]

Perumal was arrested and convicted in Finland after he tried to fix games in the local football league, the Veikkausliiga, in 2011. The reason for this somewhat obscure league being chosen by the syndicate was simple: Finland was one of the few countries that played its football during the European summer, when there was precious little else to bet on.

In the South African case, Perumal's man walked into Safa's offices with an offer that was too good to turn down. Perumal said the man was called 'Anthony' – a likely reference to Anthony Santia Raj, although Fifa investigators believed he was the match-fixer Jason Jo Lourdes. It could be that Perumal deliberately used the wrong name to confuse investigators and protect his friends who had not yet been arrested or that the Fifa investigators got the name wrong.

But Fifa and Perumal agree that a betting agent met with Safa officials that day and that he left with a deal that put Perumal in control of the referees for South Africa's five warm-up games leading up to the 2010 tournament.

In *Kelong Kings*, Perumal spells out how he went about rigging the South African friendlies: 'The South Africa World Cup friendly warm-up matches were my idea. I had thought about the scheme four years earlier, right after being released from prison. I was sitting in front of the television watching the telecast of the warm-up matches played before the World Cup in Germany. "Fuck," I thought, "there is no real football involved here. All you have to do is put two teams together and you can make big money."'

When 2010 came around, Perumal hatched a plan: '"Why don't I get my referees to officiate in the World Cup warm-up matches before the 2010 World Cup in South Africa?" I thought. "After all, it's Africa, not Europe, where there are too many questions asked and strict regulations to follow. In Africa, it can be done."'[15]

Perumal outlines how 'Anthony', after speaking to a Safa official, met with the organisation's head of referees, Steve Goddard: 'The two met and Anthony offered Goddard some money so that he wouldn't trouble us; we thought it wiser to have the head of referees in our good books.

'"Mr Goddard," proposed Anthony, "keep these three thousand dollars for your expenses. It's a goodwill gesture from our sponsor."'

To his eternal credit, Goddard turned the offer down, causing the Safa official (named as 'Jacob' in the book) to say: 'He may be head of referees, but we have the power to overrule him.'

Fifa investigators would later describe Goddard as the only Safa official who reported being offered money. 'My theory was quite simple: these guys are crooks, get them out the system,'[16] he told me.

According to Perumal, the Safa official was promised US$10 000 for every match in which Football4U was allowed to place its referees – the two assistants included – and this official began to operate as a 'front man', introducing Perumal's man to the then Safa CEO, Leslie Sedibe.

'Anthony convinced Sedibe that Safa did not need referees from Europe when there were local African match officials that could be promoted to the task.'

As usual, Football4U would cover everything – flights, accommodation and expenses.

Perumal's man convinced Sedibe, who 'liked the idea and seemed forthcoming'. Soon the rest of the management at Safa was persuaded by the continuous mention of the line, 'You know everything is coming for free.'[17]

Perumal wrote: 'Anthony and I drafted a contract saying that Football4U was going to officially supply referees for the 2010 South Africa World Cup warm-up friendly matches and Leslie Sedibe signed it enthusiastically. It was agreed that we would provide refs for the five friendly matches pitting South Africa against Thailand, Bulgaria, Colombia, Guatemala and Denmark. Job done; mission accomplished; and Anthony came back to Singapore.'[18]

A copy of the contract, signed by Sedibe on behalf of Safa, is headed: 'This agreement is made on the 11th day of May 2010 between South Africa Football Association of 125 Samuel Evans Road Aeroton Johannesburg (hereinafter referred to as 1st Party) and Football4U International Private Limited of Block 640 Rowell Road 601-58 Singapore (hereinafter referred to as the Second Party).'[19]

The agreement was simple. Safa agreed 'to use the services of the Second Party in respect of Friendly International matches scheduled to take place in South Africa from 24th May to 5th June 2010'.[20]

With Safa on board, the match-fixers worked on the other side of the deal, contracting referee teams – a referee and two assistants each – from Kenya, Togo and Niger.

Chaibou would turn out to be their shining star.

'Ibrahim had just one more year of refereeing to go before retirement when he was asked the burning question. "What are you going to do after you quit?"' 'Anthony' inquired. 'Fifa is going to give you a pension. They pay you one or two thousand dollars and fly you around business class; we give you first class and we'll pay you 60 to 70 thousand dollars per match.'[21]

'I can do the job,' Ibrahim told 'Anthony'.

From Perumal's account, some South African officials knew something was awry.

Botswana's football president, David Fani, realised something was amiss when he saw that Football4U was involved in organising the referees. Fani alerted Goddard to the fact that Football4U had approached Botswana players to fix games in China in 2009.

Goddard kept a close watch on the referees.

The first game, against Thailand on 16 May 2010, was won handsomely by South Africa, who scored four unanswered goals, but Perumal claims there was no betting interest in this game.

In the next game, against Bulgaria, on 24 May 2010, the referee was asked to deliver three goals in total, but the game ended in a 1–1 draw. Perumal sent the referee home with just US$2 000.

Perumal was determined to start making money in the next game, when South Africa took on Colombia on 27 May 2010 in the inaugural game at the rebuilt Soccer City stadium.

His handpicked match official for the occasion was Kenyan referee Samwel Langat and his two assistants. 'All we wanted were three goals, and, if the teams were so bad that they didn't manage to score on their own, we would be forced to give away penalties; even three per match. And that's exactly what Samwel did.'[22]

In the 15th minute, Langat awarded South Africa a dubious penalty for a handball. It is clear from replays that the ball was nowhere near a Colombian hand.

Astonishingly, when the Colombian keeper saved the ball, one of the assistant referees flagged, claiming the goalkeeper had moved. The penalty was retaken.[23]

In the 20th minute, the Colombians were awarded a penalty after the South African goalkeeper took out a striker in the box. A second goal was scored, but the Colombians were outraged that the keeper was only given a yellow card for what was clearly a red-card offence.

So furious were the Colombians that they threatened not to come out after half-time.

In the end they did, only to see South Africa awarded another dubious penalty in the 55th minute. The game ended 2–1, giving the betting syndicate the three goals they wanted.

As investigative journalist Declan Hill wrote in *The New York Times*: 'The stadium, indeed the entire event, was a sign that a new South Africa was ready for the international stage. It seemed to show that this was a South Africa that had emerged from apartheid to become a prosperous, multi-cultural society. It was a wonderful day for sport and society. The only problem was that the game was probably fixed.'[24]

So bad was his performance that Samwel Langat's career as a Fifa referee came to an abrupt end after just two years. According to Perumal, the syndicate paid him off handsomely.

In the fourth match, South Africa played Guatemala and, as described at the beginning of this chapter, referee Ibrahim Chaibou and his team met expectations, producing a five-goal bonanza and awarding three penalties (of which two were converted).

According to Perumal: 'After the match, Ibrahim and his officials were paid.' His associate, 'Dan', handed over US$60 000.

The clumsy meddling of Chaibou and Langat in the two penalty-riven games finally pushed Goddard to act.

Sensing that they had been rumbled, the syndicate came up with a clever strategy. They would field a Tanzanian referee who had not yet been implicated and he would pull up injured just before the game against Denmark (played on 5 June in Atteridgeville) so that Chaibou could replace him and perform his magic.

But, to Perumal's disappointment, the referee reported injured well before the game.

Then followed high farce as Goddard loaded South African referee Matthew Dyer into his car and raced to the venue to get him on to the field. When he reached the ground, Chaibou was already standing in the tunnel with the players, waiting to take the field.

Goddard told me how he, accompanied by fellow Safa official Adeel Carelse, intercepted Chaibou in the tunnel. 'We got him back into his tracksuit and took him up into the stands.'[25]

Perumal picks up the story: 'The match was about to commence: floodlights on; live telecast running; anthems ready to play; two teams lined up behind our star ref. Then suddenly, Ibrahim was pulled out and replaced by Goddard's protégé, Matthew Dyer. Once our ref was out, nothing could be done. We lost our match and one million dollars went up in smoke. We wanted three goals and instead, the match ended 1–0 in favour of South Africa. Steve Goddard, the mother-fucker.'[26]

An enraged Perumal called Goddard from his hotel room, saying: 'I am the CEO of Football4U. How dare you pull my referee out of the game? Are you aware that we have a contract in our hands that gives us the right to designate the ref for that match? ... We have a legal agreement with Safa and you do this to us? We will hold you responsible for this and sue you fuckers, especially you Steve Goddard!'[27]

In Goddard's version, he received a death threat from Perumal. 'He just said: "This time you have gone too far." He was indicating that he was going to eliminate me.'[28]

Safa generously offered Perumal the consolation of fielding his referees for the Nigeria vs North Korea friendly match on 6 June 2010 to make up for the failure of the Denmark game to net the required number of goals.

Goddard would make one final attempt to rescue the integrity of the game.

According to Perumal: 'I turned to look and saw a limping old man with a stick, the only white guy among a sea of Africans, advancing hastily towards me.'[29] Goddard approached Nigerian football officials, but, according to Perumal, he headed off Goddard's intervention by handing the Nigerians US$5 000 in cash and they laid no complaint about the referee.

Terrified after he felt his life had been threatened, Goddard filed no report on the match-fixing incidents. He told me that he did inform Fifa officials about his suspicions and left it at that.

'In the end,' commented Perumal, 'Goddard did not file any complaint and everything was hush-hush. Three of our matches had produced profits, one was un-influential and only two had backfired. Each match was worth about 1.5 million US dollars in profit, making us walk away with a good four to five million dollars.'³⁰

Exactly how Perumal ingratiated himself with Safa remains a mystery, as no formal criminal investigation has ever been conducted into the match-fixing scandal. An internal Safa report and one by Fifa were damning, but did not lead to a police investigation.

And, as one official who did not wish to be named put it to me: 'It was too good to be true. The obvious question was: What's in it for Football4U? Why would they go to all this expense? In return for what?'

Safa's spin on the match-fixing scandal has been that naïve officials from a hard-up association were presented with a life-saving plan. They should have known better, but they signed up out of ignorance.

A flood of astonishing details of how the match-fixing plans were executed was revealed as the scandal broke. Among the more colourful stories was one detailing a corrupt referee's banking transaction. *New York Times* reporters Declan Hill and Jere Longman revealed how, on the day of the Guatemala match, Chaibou was paid a handsome sum: 'Chaibou walked into a bank in a small South African city carrying a bag filled with as much as US$100 000 in $100 bills, according to another referee travelling with him. The deposit was so large that a bank employee gave Mr Chaibou a gift of commemorative coins bearing the likeness of Nelson Mandela.'³¹

That evening, Chaibou would take to the field for the Guatemala game.

Chaibou, who retired in 2011, denied any involvement in match-fixing despite a finding by Fifa that 'on the balance of probabilities' the five friendlies ahead of the World Cup were rigged.

Declan Hill added: 'However, it gets worse, much worse – in the Fifa report and separate interviews, a former South African Football Association official, Adeel Carelse, says that the connections between the fixers and key officials inside Safa carried on after the World Cup was over.'[32]

Hill wrote that in January 2011 Carelse had seen a 'potentially corrupted referee' and members of the fixing gang at a Safa function ahead of a game between Egypt's and South Africa's Under-23 teams: 'He reported his concerns to his bosses and arranged for a referee unconnected with the fixers to officiate the game. Carelse says that he was then misdirected to another stadium by a Safa official and had to drive frantically across the city to replace the referees at the last moment.'[33]

South African officials were well aware of the allegations of match-fixing, but rather than expose them to the full might of the law, they kept their knowledge to themselves.

* * *

An internal Safa report into the matter was kept secret because it was thought unwise to rain on the parade – the parade being the growing national hype over the tournament that had been bolstered by a string of Bafana victories.

It was more than a year later, on 7 October 2011, that Safa's security head, Mlungisi Ncame, and its COO, Dennis Mumble, met with Fifa security chief, Chris Eaton, at OR Tambo International Airport, to request a Fifa investigation.

Fifa's anti-corruption team, headed by Chris Eaton and Terry

Steans, investigated the claims. A year later, in October 2012, they submitted a report into 'Allegations of impropriety against some employees of the South African Football Association and other individuals in some pre-World Cup 2010 international friendly matches'. The report, which includes well over 400 pages of transcripts of the interviews conducted, raises some very serious questions about Safa's then leadership.

Safa's cooperation with the Fifa investigators was not exactly whole-hearted. The organisation agreed to arrange for the referees under suspicion to be flown to South Africa for interviews, but 'these requests were not made until two days after we arrived in South Africa and only then after long deliberation by Safa despite the instruction from their President.'[34] The countries of origin then refused to cooperate, with the exception of Tanzania, which agreed to allow its referees to be interviewed only after the investigators had left the country.

Steans and Eaton did, however, interview all the Safa officials linked to the scandal, and provided the most comprehensive account of what took place in the shadows.

They found that Wilson Raj Perumal used the cover of the Football4U company, owned by Asian gambling mastermind Dan Tan Seet Eng, to 'manipulate at least five matches and possibly more'.

'According to witness statements, match fees of unspecified amounts were paid in cash to referees, who, on each occasion, were called to a hotel to be paid by the member of the syndicate.'[35]

The report's findings on Safa officials were damning. 'At the very least, it appears Safa staff members were either easily duped or extremely foolish. There is a very real possibility, however, that some Safa staff members were involved and were corrupted.'[36]

While none of the Safa officials had admitted to being corrupted, 'there is persuasive circumstantial evidence and, when combined with the "ordinary man" test of behaviour, this inevitably leads to the conclusion that several Safa employees were complicit in a criminal conspiracy to manipulate these matches'.[37]

The report recommended that six officials be 'subject to further examination under the new Fifa Discipline/Ethics arrangements', and, it added ominously, 'given the likely commission of criminal offences by persons outside and possibly inside Safa in conspiring to and succeeding in fixing the matches under examination, that the file also be referred to the South African Police.'[38]

The six Safa officials named were:

- Leslie Sedibe, the former CEO;
- Dennis Mumble, the then COO;
- Steve Goddard, former acting head of referees;
- Lindile 'Ace' Kika, Barney Kujane and Adeel Carelse, administrative officials.

Perumal's letter about the 'referees exchange program', which got the match-fixing rolling, was dated 29 April 2010 and was addressed to Safa president Kirsten Nematandani. It referred to an earlier meeting between Nematandani and Perumal, but, when interviewed by Steans and Eaton, Nematandani 'denied having ever seen the letter or having any knowledge of its existence until it was showed to him by Chris Eaton'.[39]

They found the then Safa CEO, Sedibe, equally evasive. He had signed an agreement with Football4U, but 'denied having seen a written agreement or indeed any documentation in respect of Football4U' and he 'denied signing any document in respect of Football4U'.[40] Chris Eaton then produced the document: 'He studied it and then said that it was his signature but that he did not remember signing it, however he immediately agreed that he must have done so.'[41]

Sedibe also 'lost' his Safa laptop, which contained his records of his administrative activities during the match-fixing period. However, from the transcript of Kika's answers to the investigators' questions, it is clear that Sedibe signed off on the deal with Football4U.

Kika said: 'Leslie told me that he met with these guys, and these guys have agreed – and he has agreed – that they can work with us in terms of the matches.'[42]

Sedibe proffered the old excuse that he was a busy man and probably signed the document without thinking it through.

Other officials come out of the report just as badly. Administrator Adeel Carelse submitted a report to the investigators, which they described as 'lacking in any detail': 'For a former referee and member of the Referees Committee it is not a very professional appraisal,'[43] said the investigators. 'Mr Carelse,' said the report 'was rehearsed in what he wanted to say and how he wanted to say it.'[44]

Carelse did reveal to the investigators that his life had been threatened when he attempted to expose match-fixing. 'I am public enemy number one in this country. I have had 24 death threats.'[45]

'We had people in this country that have been killed trying to do what I've been trying to do, what you guys have been trying to do.'[46]

105

Kika admitted to having a conversation with the match-fixing agent going under the pseudonym 'Mohamed', saying he was told by Mumble to take Mohamed to see Sedibe, who then told him to go ahead with the refereeing deal.

Steans and Eaton found that Kika's story was 'devoid of detail for a man who was involved in the day-to-day organisation of these matches'.[47]

Mumble, who had brought suspicion about the match-fixing to the attention of Fifa, told the investigators, 'with hindsight he believes Football4U to have been a fraudulent operation' and that Safa and Kika became involved because they were 'naïve and saw an opportunity to find referees at no cost'.[48]

The investigators said of Mumble: 'We felt that he had more information than he gave to us. Self-preservation played a major part in his interview and in the answers he gave to our questions.'[49]

Perhaps the only official to come out of the report with some dignity intact was Steve Goddard, who was described by the investigators as 'the only Safa staff member to state that the Singaporean syndicate offered him a sum of money. He was offered R30 000. Mr Goddard turned this down. Mr Goddard was told that he was being offered the money because he was the "stopper in the deal".'[50]

Evidence of referee Ibrahim Chaibou's deposit of a large sum of US dollars, referred to earlier, came from Robert Sithole, the fourth official in the match between South Africa and Guatemala: 'He recalls seeing Ibrahim deposit a large sum of US dollars; he believes that they were US$100 bills and that the sum could have been as large as US$100 000, but he is not sure of this. Ibrahim had his money in a bag so Mr Sithole could not see how much money he had in total.'[51]

South African PSL referee Lazarus Matela, who was used by Safa to drive the foreign referees to and from the matches under investigation, told the investigators that unknown 'Indian gentlemen' had 'paid the referees in cash in the hotel and that he himself was given US$600 by the Indian gentleman in US$100 bills'.[52]

The Fifa investigators said there were large gaps in the email record supplied to them by Safa, which were suspicious. They concluded: 'The agreements presented to Safa are so very rudimentary as to be commercially laughable.'[53]

They went on to say: "Were the listed matches fixed? On the balance of probabilities, yes!"[54]

"The lack of direct evidence and the evasive and unhelpful approach to the investigation by most Safa staff, however, has resulted in a conclusion that there is insufficiently cogent evidence at this time to conclude to a criminal standard that any of the matches other than South Africa v Guatemala were fixed.'[55]

They said they expected that the South African police would be asked to investigate the matter.

The police corruption-fighting unit, the Hawks, said they were conducting a criminal investigation into the matter. It seemed that the establishment was intent on dealing with this gross ethical breach in strong terms.

Then South Africa's Sports minister, Fikile Mbalula, intervened and the Safa officials were reinstated. Mbalula flew to Switzerland to tell Fifa that it was welcome to investigate.

A Fifa media release issued after the meeting said, somewhat optimistically: 'South Africa's Sports Minister Fikile Mbalula, Safa president Kirsten Nematandani and Fifa Secretary General Jérôme Valcke reached a concrete conclusion in their meeting held today at the Home of Fifa in Zürich, a new milestone in the fight against match manipulation.'[56]

The South African government had agreed, it went on to say, to establish an 'independent judicial commission of enquiry'.

'The mandate of this judicial investigation will be limited to matters related to the case of irregularities related to friendly matches of Safa in the build-up to the 2010 Fifa World Cup.'[57]

Valcke expressed very strong views: 'It is vital that this matter which dates back to 2010 is concluded soon, with the culprits to be sanctioned in accordance with the zero tolerance policy.'[58]

The Sports minister assured everyone that it would be dealt with 'as a highest priority': 'We have made a pledge to Fifa today that we will support them and Safa to bring this to an end,'[59] concluded Mbalula.

You would think that such serious commitments made in public and then sanctified by their release in an official Fifa statement indicated that those who colluded with match-fixing would soon find themselves exposed and humiliated. You would be totally wrong. These were weasel words designed to project the appearance of ethical purity. Once they had been uttered, these commitments were simply ignored.

As Declan Hill observed: 'After this meeting, all investigations went into bureaucratic limbo until the President of South Africa, Jacob Zuma, officially announced that there would be no investigation into which Safa officials had helped the fixers. When asked the reason for this decision, Zuma's spokesman responded, "He is the President. He does not have to give his reasons, he just states his decision and that is that.'"[60]

Perhaps Zuma felt he owed football a break. In February 2010, he had to apologise for fathering his 20th child following an out-of-wedlock affair with Sonono Khoza, daughter of South African soccer's 'Iron Duke' and chairman of the World Cup organising committee, Irvin Khoza.

Zuma's announcement surprised Mbalula, who had announced the commission of inquiry. South Africa's *Sunday Times* newspaper reported that the two had attended a Bafana Bafana friendly against Brazil together and Zuma had made no mention of his intention to can the inquiry.

Zuma's then spokesman, Mac Maharaj, said: 'The international football association, Fifa, has advised the president that there is currently a pending preliminary investigation on the same matter by Fifa.'[61]

Years later, in October 2015, a fall guy was finally found. Safa's head of national teams at the time of the scandal, Lindile Kika, was suspended for six years for his part in the match-fixing scandal. A Fifa statement read: 'The adjudicatory chamber of the Ethics Committee, chaired by Hans-Joachim Eckert, has banned Lindile Kika, a former official of the South African Football Association (Safa), from all football-related activities at national and international level for six years. The ban is effective immediately.

'The proceedings against Lindile Kika were opened in November 2014 in relation to several international friendly matches played in South Africa in 2010.'[62]

Kika was found to have violated articles 13, 15, 18, 19 and 22 of the Fifa Code of Ethics.

In March 2016, three more Safa officials were sanctioned.

Despite being the only Safa official to report bribery, and despite his heroics in getting a corrupt referee out of a game just before kick-off, Steve Goddard lost his job at Safa and remained under investigation by Fifa's ethics committee: 'They accuse me of certain things and tell me I've got to go to Zürich. I have to pay my own airfare and accommodation.'[63]

Without the financial wherewithal, Goddard did not fly to Zürich and the ethics committee did not hear his defence. Frustrated that his efforts to stop the match-fixing had not been recognised, he told me: 'Do they really know what the word "ethics" means? The way they've treated me so far is disgraceful.'[64] Fifa banned Goddard and Adeel Carelse for two years.

Sedibe was banned for five years for breaching sections 13, 15 and 18 of the Fifa ethics code for failing in his 'fiduciary duties' and for not reporting breaches of the code to Fifa.

Sedibe reacted angrily to the banning, saying: 'I was neither consulted prior to the release of the provisional Fifa report nor invited to any of the meetings where the report was discussed.'[65]

Sedibe was adamant that he had demanded a full independent inquiry into the match-fixing allegations, to no avail, and that Safa had simply ignored his requests and his attempts to communicate with it. He had gone so far as to submit an application to Safa under the Promotion of Access to Information Act (PAIA) demanding access to documents and a laptop. 'To date, despite the PAIA application having been delivered directly to Mr Danny Jordaan, and his attorneys, ENSafrica, at his request, a response has not been forthcoming.'[66]

After detailing what he claimed were numerous injustices against him, including the deliberate destruction of evidence that might have supported his case by Safa, Sedibe concluded, 'a substantial injustice has been committed by Fifa and Safa'.[67]

The head of Safa's ethics committee, Poobalan Govindasamy, said of the banning of Kika: 'It was definitely the right decision for them to take and we hope it helps clean up the sport.' He explained why Safa had done nothing: 'We were not involved in the investigation because Fifa's ethics committee is an independent body.'[68]

Fifa investigator Terry Steans told me that the Fifa ethics committee's actions had been too little and too late: 'To get to the truth I feel more investigation was needed at the time of the first report and that was two years too late. I don't think the ethics committee did enough, but I guess they did all they could do. Too little too late, really. They never contacted me for any input although I did talk to Mike Garcia [former Fifa ethics investigator] about fixing in general.'[69]

He pointed out that Perumal was writing books about the match-fixing scandal and had spoken to several police forces. 'Why not the South African police?'[70]

'The people who were in power at Safa during the period were either duped or complicit. The fixers will tell who did what, and I'm sure under formal police interview more information would be forthcoming from those on the inside.

'The problem is a lot of good hard evidence will now be gone.'[71]

*   *   *

In February 2015, Perumal would claim that he played a part in fixing the qualification of five of the 32 teams that took part in the 2010 World Cup, as well as matches in the 2008 Beijing Olympic Games, the 2007 Women's World Cup and the 2008 African Cup of Nations.

In a documentary screened by the Al Jazeera television channel, Perumal said he had offered to arrange qualification for the Nigerian Football Federation in exchange for getting Football4U to organise pre-World Cup friendlies for the national team.[72] Four Kenyan players were signed up to ensure Nigeria won its penultimate qualification game on 14 November 2009. And he had arranged to pay the Mozambican football association US$100 000 if they won or drew their game with Tunisia. Kenya lost and Mozambique won, ensuring Nigeria qualified for the tournament.

Both the Nigerian and Mozambican football unions denied any knowledge 'that Perumal was a match-fixer'.[73]

Terry Steans recalls being shown Perumal's contact book: 'Perumal had 38 countries in one phone book contacts list – he had officials and players from those 38 countries.

'If you then go to his laptop and address book, there were over 50. Fifa has 209 associations ... so we are talking about a quarter of Fifa associations for one fixer,'[74] he said.

In 2011, Fifa signed an agreement with Interpol, the international police agency, to crack down on match-fixing. Two years alter, Interpol produced a report entitled 'Match-fixing in Football – Training Needs Assessment', which stated: 'Match-fixing has been reported in over 70 countries across six continents in the last twelve months alone (from 1

June 2012 to 31 May 2013). It should be noted that this is a conservative estimate.

'Fifa director of security Ralf Mutschke estimates "about 50 national leagues outside of Europe are being targeted by organized crime figures in the betting market" in January of this year.'[75]

Perumal did not restrict his activities to fixing actual matches. 'In addition to bribing players and match officials to fix matches, the syndicate was also involved in staging "ghost matches", where no match was ever played despite bookies making offerings such as the friendly advertised between the U21 teams from Turkmenistan and Maldives.'[76]

The match-fixing scandal would hurt the reputation of South African football, more so because of the lack of action against the perpetrators. Rigging the outcome of voting for the World Cup hosts, rigging the tender contracts for stadiums and rigging the pre-tournament friendlies would all take their toll on the reputation of South African football. But while these acts of 'white-collar' crime were being planned, a man had lost his life in a hail of bullets because of his opposition to the awarding of a stadium contract.

The unthinkable had happened as murder was added to the litany of 2010 World Cup crimes.

CHAPTER 7

Where the bodies are buried

'This is Africa, we don't have to close certain things because they are ugly.'

– Differ Mogale

While Wilson Raj Perumal was working out how to make millions by fixing South Africa's warm-up games, a far darker tragedy was playing out in Mbombela – previously Nelspruit – the capital of the Mpumalanga province.

The gateway to the southern part of the tourist mecca, the Kruger National Park, and situated between the two populous provinces of Gauteng and KwaZulu-Natal, Mpumalanga had the potential to become one of the new South Africa's commercial success stories. With rich, fertile soil, an abundance of coal and the country's major tourism attraction, what could possibly go wrong?

But, instead of rising to its potential, the province was dogged by one corruption scandal after the other, and its ethically challenged provincial government earned the province the nickname 'Mamparalanga'.

It was almost inevitable that the construction of a new stadium in the provincial capital would become a feasting ground for the greedy.

What was not anticipated was that hitmen would enforce the corruption with a string of murders. The BBC reported that 'at least three' murders had been tied to stadium corruption.[1] While details of two of the claimed killings are hard to come by, there is one case that has been extensively covered – the killing of the speaker of the Mbombela municipality, Jimmy Mohlala.

In January 2009, Mohlala was gunned down in KaNyamazane Township. He had gone too far by openly raising his objection to several aspects of the contracting around the Mbombela Stadium. Mohlala was about to file charges when he was killed. He had for three years campaigned against corruption in the stadium contracts.

Investigative journalist Mzilikazi wa Afrika wrote that he had received a 'frantic phone call' from Mohlala the day before Christmas in 2008. When Wa Afrika scheduled a meeting for early January, Mohlala had replied: 'If I'm still alive by then, we will.' He added the chilling line: 'They want me dead.'[2]

The story of Mohlala's battle with powerful figures in the council's executive and inside the provincial ANC is a tale of heroism, albeit one which would eventually be laced with tragedy.

The new stadium's main features were 18 orange steel supports, designed to resemble the giraffes that roam the nearby Kruger National Park, and a black and white zebra pattern over the seating area.

The local municipality came up with a name for it: 'Africa's Wildest Stadium'. It boasted: 'Of the 5 new 2010 stadiums, Mbombela is the only wholly South African designed and was constructed at the lowest per seat cost of any of the World Cup stadiums. As far as possible, only South African materials were used and the entire roof is 100% fabricated in SA.'³

Fifa was driven to flights of fancy in its description of the venue: 'Contrary to popular international belief, animals don't usually roam the urban streets in South Africa. But at the Mbombela stadium giant giraffes are indeed found in the inner city, as the stadium's roof columns towering overhead are distinctively shaped like giant orange giraffes that dominate the stadium's façade. And the wildlife theme doesn't stop there, as the spectator seating is crisscrossed black and white to resemble zebra prints, while traditional Ndebele paintings light up the stadium's meeting rooms, foyer and lounge areas.'⁴

Fifa went on to describe the stadium's corridors coloured in 'psychedelic lime green, mellow yellow, sky blue and electric orange walls that will have World Cup players reaching for their shades.'⁵

The stadium was officially opened with a World Cup warm-up match between South Africa and Thailand, which the local team won 4–0. It was one of the matches in which a betting syndicate controlled the referees. Perhaps this was a fitting send-off for a stadium in Mamparalanga.

The 41 000-seat stadium would be built at a cost of R1 billion – a lot of money, but nothing when compared to the cost of other World Cup stadiums. National and provincial government ploughed in the money, but the running costs would reside with the relatively poor Mbombela City Council. Corners would have to be cut and so they were.

In March 2006, Mohlala objected to an attempt by the municipality to buy the land on which the stadium was to be built from its owners, the Matsafeni community, for R1 – the equivalent of 6.25 US cents or

4 British pence.[6] The council's Differ Mogale signed a deal with the Matsafeni Trust. The land was estimated to be worth R48 million, but the council offered the token payment along with a promise to speed up the delivery of services to the community, which lacked proper piped water, electricity and sewerage.

When the community discovered that the trustees it had put in place to manage the land had agreed to the one-rand offer, they were angry. They took the council to the Pretoria High Court, and Judge Ntendeya Mavundla ruled in their favour, saying what the municipality was doing was no better than what settlers had done when they robbed indigenous people of their land by offering them mirrors and shiny buttons.

It was one of the ironies of post-apartheid South Africa that a democratically elected council would seek to rob people of their land. Especially so since the Matsafeni community had obtained the land in 2003 as the result of a settlement agreement to return land that had been stolen from them. In terms of that deal, over 4 500 individuals were resettled on 5 000 hectares of land for which the state paid the landowner no less than R57 million.

The trust had been established to look after the interests of the community groups that benefited from the return of their land. But the board of trustees lost the confidence of the community over the stadium land sale, which was described by Brian Spilg, SC, in a paper in the law magazine *Advocate* as 'the greatest one-sided land deal in recorded history'.[7]

In his ruling against the sale, Justice Mavundla said the Mbombela City Council was guilty of 'unethical and unconstitutional behaviour'.

Mohlala was not alone in questioning the land sale. The Minister of

Land Affairs at the time, Thoko Didiza, was reported as warning of dire consequences if the sale went ahead. What was worse, the council intended to move the community to a new home some 25 km away.

Following the scathing judgment, the Matsafeni community trustees agreed to a price of R9 million for the land.

The management of the stadium construction project required offices, so two schools were requisitioned, leaving the pupils out in the cold. Or should that be the heat? The solution that was found for the schools was to make available structures built from old shipping containers, which became unbearably hot in summer.

When a replacement school was eventually built, construction took place on a sensitive wetland with no environmental impact assessment having been done.

The construction of the stadium was the subject of frequent labour protests and 'violent clashes between police and local people angered by failure to build new schools displaced by the project', the Reuters news agency reported[8] after visiting the stadium site in October 2009.

'Failures to deliver electricity and water to Mataffin township next to the arena mean that World Cup matches could be played within sight of tin shacks where people live in sordid conditions without piped water or sewers,' the agency wrote.

In the Mataffin township close to the stadium, there was despair. 'We are not happy the World Cup is coming to South Africa,' said Sarah Shabangu, 29. Although her shack was in sight of the stadium, she had to use a pit latrine and drew water from a dirty borehole.

'Only a greedy few corrupt officials and their friends are going to benefit. The people on the ground won't get anything,' she said.

Khelina Sibuyi, 49, agreed. 'We use this water for drinking, cooking and bathing. The kids get sick and have diarrhea ... ever since they built the stadium we have been hoping for help in getting services but nothing is happening, there is no water or electricity.'

Differ Mogale, the municipality's 2010 coordinator, was quoted as saying: 'This is Africa, we don't have to close certain things because they are ugly.'

The human rights lawyer Richard Spoor, who helped the community get rid of the leaders who agreed to the R1 sale, summed it up: 'They promised a new school, they promised a new church, they promised many things ... every single one of those promises and those undertakings has been broken, they have done nothing.'[9]

The attempt to steal the land, the commandeering of the schools and the failure to deliver basic services were just one facet of the crookery around the stadium.

In January of 2007, Mohlala continued to question corruption around the deals, but also began questioning the Mbombela council's failure to deliver services. What developed was a rift between the council's management and the elected officials. The municipality's executive management, led by Jacob Dladla, simply defied 361 formal council resolutions calling them to order on the project.[10]

In February, Mohlala persuaded the council to fire Mogale, who had tried to sell the land for R1, and to take disciplinary action against Dladla, who was placed on compulsory leave.[11]

Investigative journalists Sydney Masinga and Justin Arenstein wrote how law firm Ngobe Nkosi Attorneys, who had been hired by the council to look into Dladla's dealings, had investigated the matter in

119

January 2008 and found that 'Dladla repeatedly refused to cooperate with investigators, illegally wiped the hard drive on his laptop and intimidated officials. The report also finds that Dladla failed to declare his business interests with the chairman of the Matsafeni Trust, that he routinely ignored council resolutions and refused to hold himself accountable to the council. As a result, service delivery imploded, prompting residents to rebel and march on the legislature.'[12]

Instead of supporting Mohlala, the ANC's provincial executive took the astonishing decision that he and the then mayor, Justice Nsibande, must resign and that the municipality be placed under administration. In so doing, they ignored the findings of the Ngobe Nkosi report. Mohlala refused to resign and was threatened with disciplinary action.

The *Mail & Guardian* newspaper said the Ngobe Nkosi report 'paints a damning picture of [Dladla's] activities since he was appointed municipal manager in October 2006, alleging manipulation of tenders, service delivery failures, victimisation and harassment of council employees, and failure to implement council resolutions as well as to keep the council informed on matters relating to the World Cup.'[13]

The report called for legal action against Dladla and the stadium's designers, Lefika Emerging Equity and the construction firm Basil Read.

The report said: 'There is irrefutable evidence that the parties already had a close association and that Lefika should have declared such when appointed as the professional manager at the Mbombela 2010 stadium.'[14]

'They should have recused themselves from any evaluation or bidding or any other committee related to this tender when Basil Read tendered. The only conclusion one could reach ... is that it would appear that Lefika had to ensure that Basil Read/Bouygues be appointed.'[15]

In June 2008, Mohlala continued his assault on municipal graft, criticising the land purchase and warning that officials involved would be held accountable for legal costs.

The pressure mounted on Mohlala and he was arrested on charges of the attempted rape of a 14-year-old girl. He insisted he was framed. He died before the case could be brought to trial. Was this a smear or did the whistleblower have his dark side?

In November, the ANC instructed the new mayor, Lassy Chiwayo, and Mohlala to reinstate Dladla and ordered that the disciplinary charges against Dladla be dropped.[16] Mohlala then blocked a council resolution implementing this instruction on procedural grounds.

* * *

In August 2012, long after the World Cup fans had left town, the Hawks effected two arrests in connection with tender fraud and corruption related to the construction of the Mbombela Stadium.

It was a scandal that ran deep. Among those arrested was none other than Bobby Motaung, the man in charge of the day-to-day affairs of one of the country's two top football clubs, Kaizer Chiefs, and the son of the club's founder, Kaizer Motaung. The younger Motaung was a director of Lefika Emerging Equity, which had been appointed by municipal manager Jacob Dladla in April 2006 to design the stadium.[17] He was

121

arrested at the club's Naturena estate, in the south of Johannesburg.

Motaung and Lefika's Herbert Theledi and Chris Grib were charged with forgery and fraud. The three were alleged to have forged tax compliance documents in order to become eligible to bid for the stadium contract.[18]

Mohlala claimed he could prove that Lefika had forged a government document and had committed 'bank fraud' to win the contract.[19] He had described the payment of R43 million to Lefika as a breach of the Municipal Finance Management Act.[20]

Motaung and Theledi were granted bail of R50 000 each and were instructed to have no contact with Mbombela municipal officials or to come within 500 m of the Mbombela municipal offices.[21]

Outside the court, protestors wearing T-shirts displaying the face of Mohlala were chanting: 'Who killed Jimmy?', 'What happened to Jimmy?' and 'Stop Corruption'.[22]

Exactly who was behind the alleged dodgy dealings from the council's side was the subject of its own controversy. Following an internal disciplinary hearing, the municipality's former manager, Jacob Dladla, was found guilty of, among other things, manipulating the tender adjudication process.[23] He was fired in March 2009, but the ANC in the region counteracted this by instructing councillors to support a resolution clearing Dladla of all charges. He was paid a 'golden handshake' of R1.5 million.[24]

Two months later, in October 2012, Dladla would be arrested to face charges.

To put a lid on the scandal, thugs also threatened Mbombela mayor, Lassy Chiwayo, who received a text message warning him to shut up about the scandal 'or you will go to your place in a coffin'.[25]

Mohlala had paid a heavy price for questioning two aspects of the stadium project: the awarding of contracts and the way in which the land had been acquired from the Matsafeni community.

The circumstances surrounding the murder of Jimmy Mohlala remain unresolved. Four people were arrested for the killing, but were released due to lack of evidence. Police then arrested a Mozambican going by the name of 'Josh', but he was also released for lack of evidence. He claimed in an affidavit that the orders to assassinate Mohlala came from a politician and a soccer personality.[26]

The Hawks confirmed in January 2016 – seven years after Mohlala was gunned down – that they had completed their investigation into corruption and forgery charges against Bobby Motaung and four others, and had asked the prosecuting authority to 'reconsider the reinstatement of the case after collecting the docket from the Mpumalanga regional Hawks investigators'.[27]

CHAPTER 8

A nation transfixed

'People said we would suffer financially from taking the World
Cup to Africa, but today I am the happiest man to announce that
the World Cup in South Africa was a huge financial success for
everybody – for Africa, for South Africa and for Fifa as it was the
first time ever that we have had over four billion dollars in our
accounts in a four-year cycle.'

– Sepp Blatter

Looking back now, it is almost surreal. South Africa was in a state of
high excitement. Just as it had done for the 1995 Rugby World Cup
and the 1996 Africa Cup of Nations, sport had worked its magic and
the nation was putting on its best face.

On 'Football Fridays' every second South African put on the national
strip of Bafana Bafana – or any other national team if the football strip
wasn't around – and embraced the World Cup.

Along with the 'Fly the Flag' programme, which saw tens of thousands of national flags fluttering from car windows or draped along
with the flags of other competing nations across office ceilings, Football
Fridays were pure marketing genius.

To give the campaign a push, government wrote to the country's top 50 corporations, asking them to play their part, and they duly obliged. Soon buildings were covered in World Cup-supporting banners.

As the fever grew, a national discussion occurred over that uniquely South African football accessory, the vuvuzela – a plastic trumpet capable of an ear-splitting bellow, usually in concert with several thousand others. It was sometimes described as South Africa's 12th man. Some 800 000 vuvuzelas were sold in South Africa, with a further 200 000 sold abroad – 40 000 of them in the UK.

The vuvuzela became the object of global scrutiny after the World Cup, with some football associations taking the step of banning them from their games.

On the eve of the tournament, a concert was held at Soweto's Orlando Stadium. Some 30 000 spectators crammed into the venue for the three-hour event, which was broadcast live. Among them was Fifa secretary-general Jérôme Valcke, the man who had pestered South Africa to cough up the US$10 million to Jack Warner, who said, 'We are thrilled to have a concert of such magnitude and performing talent rise the curtain on the first Fifa World Cup on African soil.'[1]

The concert was opened by President Jacob Zuma and Fifa's Sepp Blatter. The latter said: 'Fifa is very proud to be in South Africa, and I am very proud to be tonight in Soweto. Football is not only a game; football is connecting people.'

For his part, Zuma stuck to the by now tedious assertion that South Africa had confounded the 'Afro-pessimists' by saying: 'We would like to thank Fifa for taking this decision to host the first World Cup on

African soil. Africa is showing the world that it is capable of handling any matter of the world, like all other regions.'[2]

Football luminaries such as former South African captain Lucas Radebe, Germany's Franz Beckenbauer, Brazil's Socrates and Nigeria's Jay-Jay Okocha took to the stage.

The star turn came from an ageing Archbishop Desmond Tutu, who said: 'I have been to a lot of concerts but I have never been to a concert like this. It is amazing fun, we are having a huge jam. It is a perfect presentation of Africa – north, south, east and west.'[3]

The star performers included the Black Eyed Peas, with frontman will.i.am shouting 'South Africa, South Africa, are you ready?' They performed their hits, including the classics 'Where Is the Love' and 'I Got a Feeling'. The pop sensation of the day, Shakira, performed the official World Cup song, 'Waka Waka (This Time for Africa)'.

But tragedy struck that night. Nelson Mandela's great-granddaughter, Zenani Mandela, died in a car accident while returning from the World Cup concert, just two days after she turned 13.

The nation was still absorbing this terrible news when the big day, years in the making, finally came.

In Sandton, tens of thousands packed the streets to send off the home team, Bafana Bafana, ahead of their opening game against Mexico.

Around Soccer City, outside Soweto, the traffic backed up for kilometres as 90 000 spectators streamed in to watch the first game. The atmosphere was one of national celebration as hooters were tooted and smiling passengers greeted one another. The stadium filled to capacity and soon there was the unmistakable sound of thousands of vuvuzelas blasting in celebration as the players took to the field to warm up.

I pinched myself as I sat high in the stand, soaking up the experience of a lifetime. There are no words to describe the atmosphere of shared happiness that South Africans from all walks of life enjoyed on that day, although it must be noted that the high ticket prices had put the games out of reach of the sport's most ardent local supporters. The cheapest tickets – situated behind the goals – sold for between R140 and R1 050, depending on the gravity of the game. The most expensive seats adjacent to the pitch went for R6 300.[4] It did feel as if many in the crowd were there for the event and not for the football. They had the money to pay to witness a spectacle.

Even so, getting tickets to the games took more than a fat wallet. Fans had to apply to Fifa. The applications were held until a draw in April 2010, when the final allocation was decided.

Those who didn't have the money gathered at 'fan parks', the popular name for the Fifa-approved Public Viewing Areas (PVAs) set up in public open spaces. The fan parks in Soweto and Johannesburg had space for 75 000 spectators each. There was even a fan park in Mexico City, where 50 000 gathered to watch the opening game.

The opening ceremony took a full 40 minutes and involved 1 500 performers, including Hugh Masekela, the Nigerian singer Femi Kuti and the R&B star R Kelly.

Mandela was supposed to be the star, but he was in mourning following his great-granddaughter's death and could not attend. Blatter and Zuma took centre stage alongside VIP guests Desmond Tutu, UN secretary-general Ban Ki-Moon and the Mexican president Felipe Calderón.

Blatter said in his speech to the crowd: 'The Fifa World Cup is in

South Africa. Thank you. Congratulations to the African population, thank you to South Africa that we can stage this World Cup here. A dream came true even if he's not here tonight, but the spirit of Mandela is in Soccer City.'[5]

Zuma delivered a message from Mandela: 'Let me convey the message from our icon, who wanted to be with us to greet you before the start of the match but unfortunately there was a tragedy in the Mandela family. But he said the game must start, you must enjoy the game.' Then, to massive applause, he continued: '... I declare the 2010 Fifa World Cup open!'[6]

The tension was high, but the vuvuzelas quieted down after a goalless first half. Bafana's game against Mexico was threatening to end in the disappointment of a draw.

Then came the moment. With 53 minutes on the clock, Siphiwe Tshabalala unleashed a miraculous shot off his left foot from outside the box. When it hit the back of the Mexican net, the crowd was sent into a frenzy.

The euphoria rose to a crescendo as Tshabalala and his teammates celebrated with a pre-rehearsed dance at the corner flag.

The South African football public believed their team had finally arrived on the big stage. And they had, until Mexico's Rafael Márquez equalised with 11 minutes to go for the game to end in a draw.

Later that evening, Cape Town had its turn.

'Tonight, the beautiful new Green Point Stadium glistens and is ready to host the match of France vs Uruguay in the night leg of the opening day's matches. A beautiful sight in a beautiful setting.' These were the words that Chuck Blazer wrote in his blog, 'Travels with Chuck Blazer and his Friends ...', on the opening day of South Africa's 2010 World Cup. He had reason to be happy. By then his wallet had been fattened by the first of three payments from Warner in exchange for his vote back in 2004 in favour of South Africa hosting the tournament.

After the draw against Mexico, it was downhill for the home team. A loss to Uruguay, whose star, Diego Forlán, would go on to win the tournament's Golden Boot award, effectively sealed their fate. A game 2-1 victory in Bloemfontein over a French team in total disarray due to internal dissension was not enough to rescue the team.

The organisers' worst fear had come true: the home team was out in the first round. But South Africans did not abandon the tournament, instead adopting Ghana and other African teams and continuing to ensure sell-out crowds at almost all games, to the delight of the ticket-sellers.

The ritual of boarding special trains put on at no cost for spectators or riding the brand-new buses of the recently launched Bus Rapid Transit System became a shared national experience as the country seized on the World Cup with a fervour beyond Fifa's wildest dreams.

The opening day was the product of years of preparation, the spending of vast amounts of state money and some extraordinary compromises. The South African government embraced the World Cup with open arms and proceeded to go out of its way to satisfy Fifa's every whim with a surprising determination.

Government had a reputation for failing to deliver basic services and for public service inefficiency. But, for the tournament, all the bad habits were shelved and a newfound can-do spirit took over. The government committed R30 billion 'to major infrastructure investment programmes meant to ensure the success of the tournament', of which, it said in its mammoth '2010 Fifa World Cup Country Report', it had spent only R28 billion.[7]

But it was more than just a massive financial commitment. The World Cup required that South Africa create a huge bureaucracy to plan and execute the event, and that it hand over a huge slice of its sovereignty to Fifa.

* * *

Once the bid had been awarded in 2004, the leviathan was born. An Organising Association Agreement (OAA) was signed between Safa and Fifa, establishing the legal framework that committed Safa – with the government as guarantor – to organising and staging the 2009 Fifa Confederations Cup and the 2010 Fifa World Cup. (The Confederations Cup is a smaller tournament that is played one year ahead of the World Cup to test the readiness of the host country in a real contest.)

The responsibility was delegated to the Organising Committee of Safa, which was incorporated on 29 August 2005 in terms of Section 21 of the Companies Act. Approved as a tax-exempt public benefit organisation, its CEO was Danny Jordaan, the man who later pleaded with Fifa to pay Jack Warner the US$10 million out of funds owed to South Africa.

The Organising Committee was divided into ten sections, and a board was established with a chairman and no fewer than 27 'independent non-executive directors' and the chief executive, who was executive director of the board. The 27 board members were drawn from football, business, the legal profession, labour unions, politics and government.

The board created seven committees: an executive committee, as well as others dealing with finance and procurement; remuneration; legacy and legal; audit and risk; marketing and communications; and cost monitoring.

It wasn't all bureaucracy. Fifa's World Cup rituals ensured that there was a regular rollout of World Cup preparatory material. A logo was designed, which was described as being 'unique, vibrant and dynamic, graphically encapsulating the richness of the African continent while also drawing on South Africa's own rich and colourful heritage for inspiration'.

'The figure in the graphic represents the early rock art paintings for which our country is famous. Caught in mid-action performing a bicycle kick, this figure reflects the flair of African football; this is a simple but energetic movement that illustrates passion for the beautiful game. The symbolic kicking up of the football issues an open invitation from Africa to other nations of the world to join the game.'[8]

The football that was the subject of the bicycle kick was described, somewhat incongruously, as suggesting 'for the first time ever, this ball will touch African soil'. Even the typeface used was described as significant because it was 'acknowledging the idea that in South Africa we do things uniquely. It is playful, innocent and free-spirited. It is also bold, welcoming and friendly.'[9] Some marketing company had no doubt been handsomely rewarded for writing this nonsense.

In November 2007, an official poster was produced depicting Africa morphing into a face looking upwards at a headed football against a bright yellow background.

Then there was the mascot, which was given the name 'Zakumi'. A leopard with short green dreadlocks, he was even given an assumed personal history. 'He celebrated his 16th birthday on June 16, 2010 when South Africa played a Group A match against Uruguay.'[10] Apparently capturing the South African zeitgeist, 'Zakumi's personality is described as jolly, self-confident, adventurous, spontaneous, and he is actually quite a shrewd little fellow. He loves to perform and always follows his instinct and intuition. Zakumi is a warmhearted and caring leopard.'[11]

Kids were crazy about Zakumi, who was mobbed at public appearances.

Then came the unveiling of the tournament football, dubbed 'Jabulani', which was described as the 'roundest ever' football because it was 'designed as a result of years of scientific excellence'. There was more marketing nonsense: the ball's 11 colours were supposed to symbolise 'the 11 tribes in South Africa and the 11 players in a football team'.[12]

Meanwhile, a 'Government Coordinating Unit' was summoned into existence in August 2005.

Its job was simple: to ensure that the entire administration complied with Fifa's requirements, although it also said it wanted to 'leverage' the event for the benefit of the country and to 'create a memorable experience for fans' as well as a 'lasting legacy for South Africa and the African continent'.

No fewer than 17 'guarantees' were signed by national government and the nine host cities to provide 'all requested assistance and support in matters which related to the conduct of the competition and the operation and running of the stadia and training grounds, with a particular emphasis on match days'.[13]

A swathe of laws, amendments and regulations quietly made their way through Parliament to ensure that Fifa and its sponsors would occupy a bubble free from legal or administrative intrusion in the lead-up to and after the tournament.

In 2006, the Special Measures Act was passed, as well as a Memorandum of Understanding between the Minister of Finance and Fifa's president 'that dealt with tax matters'. To ensure that no Fifa official or sponsor would suffer the indignity of being taxed on visiting the country, amendments were passed to the VAT Act of 1991, Income Tax Act of 1962 and Customs and Excise Act of 1964.

To make absolutely sure, the National Treasury signed a guarantee 'which provided high-level administrative assistance to Fifa and nominated a single point of contact for Fifa to coordinate all tax exemption matters'.

Among the things covered in these laws and arrangements was that 'there were no restrictions on the import and export of all foreign currencies to and from the country as well as unrestricted exchange and conversion of these currencies into US dollars, euros or Swiss francs for those involved in, or attending, the tournament'.

The South African Reserve Bank was called into action to 'facilitate the provisions of the guarantee' and to ensure that Fifa's accommodation arm, Match, could bill in US dollars.

'The National Treasury, the SARS and the SARB worked closely together and developed an event-specific manual to deal with the processes and procedures on tax, VAT and customs.[14]

Beyond the nitty-gritty of foreign exchange and taxes, government signed a declaration of undertaking that 'all three spheres of government would provide support in preparing and ensuring the successful hosting of the 2010 Fifa World Cup'.

Amendments were made to the Merchandise Marks Act 'for the protection of all Fifa-registered words and logos, including the official emblem, as trademarks'.[15] Government declared the World Cup a 'protected event' in terms of Section 75(a) of the Act from 25 May 2006 until six months after 11 June 2010.

No fewer than seven pieces of legislation covering and protecting the intellectual property rights of the World Cup were passed or amended. These included the:

- Trade Marks Act, 1993
- Designs Act, 1993
- Copyright Act, 1978
- Merchandise Marks Act, 1941
- Trade Practices Act, 1976
- Counterfeit Goods Act, 1997
- Special Measures Act, 2006.

And, to make absolutely sure than no official sponsor was deprived of their position in the limelight, 'regulations on the prohibition of the use of certain words, devices, letters, emblems and numerals for the 2010 Fifa World Cup were published on 21 June 2007 in the *Government Gazette'*.[16] These regulations were also applicable from 25 May 2006 until six months after the start of the World Cup, on 11 June 2010.

Fifa was jealously guarding the revenue it would get from the headline sponsors of the event – Adidas, Coca-Cola, Visa and other global corporate giants. It went further, establishing a 'Rights Protection Programme' to prevent so-called ambush marketing. Government devoted some time to explaining exactly how 'ambush marketing' could hurt a sponsor: 'Ambush marketing could take either of two forms, namely "association" and "intrusion". By means of "association", the ambush marketer misleads the public into thinking that he is an authorised sponsor or contributor associated with the event.

'By means of "intrusion", the ambush marketer promotes his own brand through the medium of the publicity attracted by the event and without the authorisation of the event organiser.'[17]

There was more. A 'National Rights Protection Committee', which included the Department of Trade and Industry, Fifa and the organising committee, was established to look after Fifa's commercial rights. Other government departments were mobilised to support the initiative.

At the borders, R630 million was spent on 'immigration information technology systems' and a total of R3 billion was spent on new infrastructure.

Concerned that South Africa's notoriously high crime rate would make an awkward appearance at the tournament, government left no stone unturned. Some 40 000 new police officers were incorporated into the South African Police Service to assist with the implementation of a R1.3 billion operational security plan.

The security plan included the purchase of six Robinson helicopters, four command vehicles, ten water cannons, 4x4 vehicles and 'crowd management and satellite imaging equipment'.[18] Armed safety and security officers would accompany the Fifa delegation, media representatives and 'all accredited persons before, during and after matches and while travelling in the country'. The teams, referees and Fifa delegation were given official police escorts. Four police officers were allocated to each participating team. Between 850 and 1 000 officers patrolled the trains taking fans to and from venues each day.

The Department of Justice upgraded 56 courts dedicated to the World Cup, recruited 1 140 dedicated court officials, 'including magistrates, prosecutors, attorneys, paralegals and interpreters', and trained 290 unemployed youths as ushers.[19] 'The primary objective of the Administration of Justice project was to fast track all criminal matters resulting from the 2009/2010 events and deal with cases in a fast and efficient way, especially where foreigners were involved as complainants, witnesses or the accused.'[20]

Unsurprisingly, crime during the tournament was at an all-time low and South Africans had never felt safer on the streets. The courts heard just 222 cases – about four cases per court or one case per five court officials.

Afterwards, government boasted: 'The provision of safety and security during the tournament was a resounding success, substantially demonstrated by the fact that only 290 crimes (thefts only) were reported during the 64 matches attended by 3 082 514 fans. Between 25 000 and 50 000 [police] members were deployed on a daily basis and no serious crimes were reported in the fan parks, PVAs, on any forms of transport, at team base camps or training venues.'[21]

The country's normally ponderous labour laws were brushed aside. When private security guards went on strike at several prominent stadiums on the eve of the tournament, they were summarily fired and replaced by police officers – a process that usually took weeks and months of labour relations hearings.

A 'Border Control Operational Coordinating Committee' was established to smooth the movement of arriving fans. OR Tambo, Cape Town, Polokwane and Lanseria airports were all upgraded while the brand-new King Shaka International Airport was built at La Mercy, outside Durban. Other ports of entry with neighbours were also upgraded – Lebombo, Golela, Vioolsdrift and Skilpadhek.

The infrastructure implications of the project were numerous. In Polokwane the water treatment works had to be doubled in size. The Department of Communications spent some R996 million on new communications infrastructure. The Department of Transport bought 520 new buses and recruited 1 005 new drivers. Extra trains were laid on for Polokwane, Rustenburg, Bloemfontein and Nelspruit, while host cities implemented what were described as 'citywide and event-venue transport management plans, including temporary park-and-ride services and event shuttles, road restrictions, road closures and traffic management'.[22]

The Department of Tourism intervened in the accommodation market to ensure that 'hotel prices for the Fifa delegation and commercial affiliates, broadcasters and media teams would be frozen from 1 January 2010 and that the prices would be 20% less than the frozen prices'.[23]

The Second Special Measures Act was promulgated by the Department of Health to ensure that 'there would be no restrictions imposed on the Fifa family regarding the marketing, distribution, serving, consuming and advertising of alcoholic beverages'.[24]

Even the Department of Arts and Culture got in on the act, verifying foreign national symbols and ensuring that the right anthems were played before matches. It trained 250 'protocol officers' to ensure that the dignitaries were treated with the proper respect. 'It also developed a flag and national anthem "bank", ensuring that the required standards were met, both at matches and for city "dressing".'[25]

The Department of Energy was tasked with 'commissioning, installing, operating and decommissioning temporary power generators at all the host stadia and the two broadcasting compounds.'[26] Eight projects aimed at 'strengthening the grid' in host cities were undertaken.

South Africa's notoriously vigorous Competition Commission was cowed into submission. 'The oil industry sought, and was granted, a temporary exemption from relevant sections of the Competitions Act, 1998, by the Competition Commission. This enabled the oil companies to work together in planning, coordinating and executing the necessary actions.'[27]

The National Disaster Management Centre spent R700 000 on the training of 172 specially selected firefighters as hazardous materials technicians. 'Three emergency numbers were published and 745 fire services personnel were trained and deployed to all host cities. The host cities acquired 55 firefighting engines for the event.'[28]

A key focus was the construction of stadiums. This, of course, necessitated a junket to visit stadiums in Frankfurt, Munich and Berlin 'as part of the study tour to learn and understand the complexities with particular reference to Fifa requirements for match venues.'[29]

All of this for one month of football.

* * *

On 11 July 2010, Spain played the Netherlands in the final game at Soccer City.

The match, which was played in the evening, was preceded by a 30-minute closing ceremony. Beamed live to an estimated 215 countries and territories and watched by some 500 million viewers, the closing ceremony was performed by 780 cast members. Shakira, joined by local outfit Freshlyground, gave one last performance of 'Waka Waka', which topped the charts in 15 countries and was the most watched video on the internet in June, with over 70 million hits on YouTube. Ladysmith Black Mambazo, Jozi, Abigail Kubeka, Nigeria's 2Face and Ghana's Samini also performed.

In the end, all was forgiven and Franz Beckenbauer, one of the architects of Germany's victory in the dirty 2006 bid, was described by government as 'one of football's greatest heroes'. He said: 'I think the whole world is talking about South Africa, how beautiful the World Cup has been. Everything has worked and you will see after many years the world will be talking about the World Cup in South Africa, so that's the legacy.'[30] The irony was thick. He was right, but for the wrong reasons.

Then came the moment of the day, and perhaps of the tournament. An ailing Nelson Mandela was driven on to the field in a golf cart. Wearing a winter hat and jacket against the near-freezing temperatures, he was driven around the stadium as the spectators rose in a frenzy of cheering. It was to be his last ever appearance at a public event.

The great and the good were present. Alongside the Dutch and Spanish royal families in the stands were the South African Hollywood sensation, Charlize Theron, President Jacob Zuma, the Spanish singer Placido Domingo, the tennis star Rafael Nadal and actor Morgan Freeman, who had played Mandela in the film about the 1995 Rugby World Cup, *Invictus*.

The game was, as finals often are, a damp squib. No fewer than 14 yellow cards were issued – nine of them to the Netherlands – by referee Howard Webb. The Netherlands' John Heitinga was red-carded and many thought that his teammate, Nigel de Jong, was lucky not to suffer the same fate after kicking Spain's Xabi Alonso in the chest. Webb later said he would have given the second red card had his view not been obstructed.

With four minutes to go in extra time, Spain's Andrés Iniesta smashed a half volley past Dutch goalkeeper Maarten Stekelenburg to seal victory.

When the referee blew the final whistle, the Spanish players celebrated, then they changed their blue away jerseys for red ones, with a World Cup star already placed above the badge.

Dutch football legend Johan Cruyff tore a strip off his national team for playing 'in a very dirty fashion', describing the final as 'ugly', 'vulgar' and 'anti-football'. He criticised Webb for not sending off more players.[31]

As a footballing spectacle, the 2010 World Cup had not lived up to expectations, some said because the Jabulani ball was too perfect – it had no swerve. But, as a giant, feel-good, rolling party for middle-class South Africa and the foreign fans who poured into the country, it was a great success. And, as a moneymaking machine for Fifa, it succeeded beyond the wildest imaginings of Blatter and Valcke.

Blatter would say in the foreword to Fifa's financial report on the 2010 event, released a year later: 'Thanks to the conservative and careful financial policies that we followed in the 2007–2010 period, we have been able to considerably increase our investment in football development programmes, and in 2010, we were able to give each member association a total extraordinary FAP [Financial Assistance Programme] payment of USD 550 000 and each confederation USD 5 million.' In other words, so much money was made that a bonus was paid back to officials and confederations. Blatter was always careful to share a small slice of the loot with the federations that kept him in office.

The capacity of Fifa to own the marketing space for its sponsors had not gone unnoticed and Blatter's till would ring into the future. 'I am delighted that even before this cycle drew to a close, we were able to conclude long-term contracts with many existing as well as new partners. This proves that although we are in challenging financial times, multinational companies still seek to identify with football in general and with the Fifa World Cup™ in particular. All of this fills me with great optimism and confidence for the period that lies ahead.'[32]

In the same report, the chair of Fifa's finance committee, Julio H Grondona, said: 'South Africa thrilled fans all around the world with an impeccably organised and colourful World Cup as well as with their incredible hospitality. The stadiums were virtually sold out (to 97% capacity) and the sponsors were delighted, which ensured that the tournament was a financial success for Fifa and the LOC. Fifa closed the 2007–2010 period with a result of USD 631 million and also increased its reserves to USD 1 280 million.'

The financial report explained how Fifa had made its money: 'In terms of event-related revenue of USD 3 890 million, USD 2 448 million was attributable to the sale of television rights, of which the lion's share – USD 2 408 million – were for the 2010 Fifa World Cup South Africa™. The second-biggest source of income was the sale of marketing rights worth USD 1 097 million, of which USD 1 072 million was generated by the Fifa World Cup™. The sale of hospitality rights generated USD 120 million and licensing rights USD 71 million. Other event-related income was made up primarily of revenue from the Fifa Club World Cup, which was matched, however, by comparable costs.'[33]

Sepp Blatter was ecstatic. *Fifa World* – the organisation's newsletter – quoted him as saying: 'People said we would suffer financially from taking the World Cup to Africa, but today I am the happiest man to announce that the World Cup in South Africa was a huge financial success for everybody – for Africa, for South Africa and for Fifa as it was the first time ever that we have had over four billion dollars in our accounts in a four-year cycle.'[34]

In today's money, Fifa took home US$10 billion from the 2010 event.

You could take the view that the South African government incurred a debt of R28 billion so that Fifa could make a profit of R10 billion. A more generous view would hold that South Africa 'invested' the R28 billion in building goodwill, which would pay off in what its politicians call 'social cohesion' and in future tourism and investment.

The government's view was that 'South Africa has always viewed the hosting of the World Cup not as an end in itself, but as a catalyst for developing the benefits of which would be felt long after the tournament. That is why national government has spent R30 billion on transportation (roads, airports and ports of entry), telecommunications infrastructure, as well as stadia.'[35]

Fikile Mbalula, the Sports minister, said, in the foreword to the government's 2010 report: 'The organisation and staging of the World Cup was a resounding success that left a tangible feeling of pride in all South Africans. In fact, at the conclusion of the event the Fifa president awarded South Africa "nine out of ten" as hosts. Equally vocal about the positive outcome were the national and international sports media, many of the visiting football fans from around the globe and prominent world leaders and opinion makers – all showered South Africa with accolades and some even labeled the event "the best World Cup ever".'[36]

South Africa had, he said, 'raised the bar and set a new benchmark' for the staging of the World Cup.[37]

In the short term, the payoff was significant. Some 309 554 visitors are said to have entered South Africa in 2010 because of the World Cup alone, generating revenue of R3.64 billion.

Government claims that average spending by tourists in 2010 was R11 800 – up from R9 500 in 2009 and R8 400 in 2008.

The total number of international 'Non Africa' visitors to the country in 2010 was recorded as rising from 242 155 in 2009 to more than double, at 571 642, for 2010. African visitors rose from 877 249 in 2009 to 1 814 149 in 2010.[38]

In all, some 3.1 million spectators were recorded for the 64 matches, 'the third-highest aggregate attendance behind the United States in 1994 and Germany in 2006'.[39]

The claimed economic impact can also not be ignored. In the

government's words, 'The R11.7 billion investment in 10 excellent stadia alone created 66 000 new construction jobs, generating R7.4 billion in wages, with R2.2 billion going to low-income households and therefore contributing to a reduction in poverty.'[40]

It goes without saying that upgrades to railway stations, roads and airports are here to stay. But it is hard to put a value on the global attention that was focused on South Africa. In Spain, some 13.4 million people tuned in for the final match, while 8.5 million watched in the Netherlands. When Germany played Spain in the semifinals, 32 million Germans are said to have watched on television. There was a claimed average audience of 70 million per game in the 217 countries and territories to which they were broadcast.

It was the first World Cup where social media played a large role, and government claimed in the 2010 report that 'The World Cup final represented the largest period of sustained activity for an event in Twitter's history.' Apparently some 12 million internet visitors per minute were recorded towards the end of the opening match, breaking the previous record set by the election of Barack Obama as US President, when 8.5 million visitors per minute were recorded.

The local organising committee claimed it had made a 'profit' from the event. It had earned income of US$526 million of which US$226 million was paid as 'direct support from Fifa' and a further US$300 million was earned in ticket revenue, which Fifa passed on to it. Operational expenses amounted to a total of US$516 million 'resulting in an anticipated profit of US$10 million'.

It seems churlish to pour cold water on the excitement and the claimed benefits of the 2010 World Cup, an event that all South

Africans remember with fondness as a time of national unity and as a celebration of success.

But, five years later, the vast amounts spent on the stadiums, several of which were fully used only for the month of the tournament, seem ludicrously high. We now know that that is in part due to crooked business practices that have since been exposed. Municipalities now bear much of the financial burden of these white elephants and it is with no small amount of irony that, subsequent to the World Cup, Danny Jordaan was appointed mayor of Nelson Mandela Bay municipality in the Eastern Cape – one of the country's poorest metros, and one that is saddled with paying for its underutilised stadium.

In addition to the construction debt that has been visited on future generations, the goodwill generated by the event has all but vanished amid the claims of match-fixing and vote-rigging during the bid. And, six years after the edifying display of national unity, the country appears to be descending into a bitter crisis over racism.

CHAPTER 9

Spinning out of control

'When we organised the World Cup we were dealing with people, not gangsters. The fact that they later turn into gangsters in not our problem.'

– Fikile Mbalula

After piecing together the events that led to Jack Warner and his fellow Concacaf executives changing their vote to support South Africa's bid to host the 2010 World Cup, I composed a list of questions for former President Thabo Mbeki. These were:

1. When, where and by whom was the promise made to pay US$10 million towards the diaspora in the Caribbean?

2. Did you attend any meeting with Warner and/or Chuck Blazer where a payment of this kind was discussed? Was this matter discussed at the meeting held between yourself, Mr Mandela, Mr Warner and Mr Blazer at the Dolder Grand Hotel in Zürich on the morning of 14 May 2004, a day before the vote? Was it discussed in the subsequent 'private meeting' between yourself, Mr Warner and Mr Blazer on the same morning?

3. Why did the South African government not pay the money as promised?

4. Why did Safa insist that the money be under the fiduciary control of Jack Warner?

5. Why was there no public statement about the undertaking to pay the money or the actual payment of the money?

6. What, in your view, changed Jack Warner's mind about voting for South Africa in the run-up to the May 2004 vote?

Mbeki's spokesman, Mukoni Ratshitanga, responded: 'As you may be aware, former President Mbeki's Office issued a statement on May 29 last year which dealt with the 2010 Fifa World Cup bribery allegations.

'I share the statement below for your reference. We can neither add nor subtract from the statement.'

The statement read:

> As former President of the Republic of South Africa, I have noted reports alleging that bribes were solicited and paid to some officials of the Fédération Internationale de Football Association (Fifa) in exchange for our country to host the 2010 Soccer World Cup.
>
> I am not aware of anybody who solicited a bribe from the Government for the purpose of our country being awarded the right to host the World Cup. As Minister of Sport and Recreation, Fikile Mbalula, has stated on behalf of the Government, no public money was ever used to pay a bribe.
>
> I wish to state that the Government that I had the privilege to lead would never have paid any bribe even if it were solicited.

> It is therefore unnecessary for me or my office to make further
> comments on this matter.[1]

It goes without saying that this statement offers no serious answer to the questions I had raised.

A set of questions along the same lines for Danny Jordaan elicited a similar response from his chief of staff, Mlungisi Ncame: 'Dr Jordaan is of the view that these questions were addressed extensively by the Minister of Sport, Hon Mr Fikile Mbalula and the DG, Mr Alex Moemi, at a press conference convened at Safa house specifically for this purpose in 2015.'[2]

An answer was offered for only one of the questions. I had asked why Jordaan had not travelled to Zürich for the executive meeting held after arrests of Fifa officials in May 2015. Ncame responded: 'Dr Jordaan did not travel to Zurich because he had to attend to council business.'[3]

Jordaan had been scheduled to attend the meeting, but pulled out at the last moment, leading to speculation that he was afraid he might be arrested in connection with the bribe allegations. Jordaan also failed to attend the Fifa Extraordinary Congress, which elected a new president in Zürich in February 2016, possibly for the same reason.

With none of the key players willing to answer questions, I turned to the public statements already on the record.

The first response to the bribe allegations against South Africa had come from South Africa's Sports minister, Fikile Mbalula. A colourful personality who is prone to outrageous public statements, his reaction was predictably full of bluster: 'We reject these falsehoods with the contempt they deserve. As a government and people of South Africa we are enjoined to combat such propaganda against our country. Accordingly, we appeal to all our people, media included, to desist from speculating on names of individuals who may or may not be implicated in the allegations,' he said.[4]

'We view this as an attack on our sovereignty,' he continued.[5]

'We affirm our position that no public funds have been utilised to pay any bribe or to commit any unlawful acts,' Mbalula said.

He was right. As we have seen, the money was not paid by the government or by Safa, but was – on the instruction of South African football officials – deducted from funds to be paid to the country by Fifa.

Understandably, attention turned to Safa.

It took nine days for South Africa's football bosses to get their act together after the stunning revelations of 27 May 2015.

The Fifa indictment had detailed two serious allegations of corruption that required a response. The first was that a member of the Local Organising Committee (LOC) had handed over a briefcase containing stacks of US dollar bills to one of Jack Warner's sons at a Paris hotel.

The second was that, under the cover of an 'African diaspora' fund, US$10 million had been paid into accounts controlled by Warner. Warner had used the money for personal ends and to pay Chuck Blazer some US$750 000 in compensation for his part in the rigging of the voting for the 2010 World Cup.

When Safa's response was eventually placed on the public record, on 6 June 2015, it ran to several pages and amounted to an outright denial of any wrongdoing by any of its officials. The allegations were, it said, 'false'.

Curiously, the first section of the response was essentially a political argument. 'The association is alarmed by the narrative that has developed around its strong support for the South African Government African Diaspora in the World Cup legacy projects, specifically the Caribbean.'[6]

The statement expressed concern that this new narrative was wrong because it 'casts the country's inclusion of the African Diaspora as morally wrong, sinister and therefore criminal in nature' and 'insinuates that leaders in the then local organising committee and the government conspired to bribe their way to Fifa World Cup in South Africa'.[7]

This political feint begs the obvious question: if the African Diaspora Legacy Programme was such an important political statement, why had the government made no mention of it in any of its official documentation around the World Cup?

Why had the money been paid quietly in three tranches from a Fifa account in Zürich on the instructions of South African officials? Where was the publicity that would normally accompany such a massive donation, especially one of which the donor was proud?

The Department of Sport and Recreation had issued a 204-page document entitled '2010 Fifa World Cup Country Report' after the tournament, in which it bragged about South Africa's achievements. Strangely, it made no mention of the diaspora legacy fund at all. In his foreword to the document, Fikile Mbalula wrote of the 2010 World Cup as 'an African event, one that could spark confidence and prosperity across the continent and hail a new century of growth and development in Africa'. Hosting the World Cup required, he said, 'close cooperation between South Africa and her sister countries in

150

Africa, calling upon the central assets of the continent: the warmth, friendliness, humility and humanity of her people.'[8]

Safa's statement said that the reason that there had been no mention of the 'African Diaspora Legacy' programme in official documentation was that it fell under the programme for Africa. 'We were also reminded by Minister Mbalula that the African Union views the African Diaspora as one of its six regions. It should therefore come as no surprise that the African Diaspora was included in the benefits of the first Fifa World Cup held on African soil.'[9]

A substantial section of the 2010 Fifa World Cup Country Report was devoted to the World Cup legacy programmes. Not a word was written about the diaspora legacy programme although space was devoted to a programme called 'Win in Africa with Africa', which included work that had taken place in Tanzania, Ethiopia, Mali, Madagascar and Mauritius. This was odd considering the size of the financial contribution to the 'diaspora'.

The statement continued its argument, saying that, 'The presence of the African Diaspora in the programme of the Fifa World Cup is further recognised in the statement of Dr Irvin Khoza, the Chairman of the 2010 Local Organising Committee (the LOC), during the launch of the 2010 Fifa World Cup slogan 'Ke Nako' on 26 November 2007.'

On that occasion, Khoza had said: 'Ke Nako simply means "It's Time". And indeed Africa's time has come to use the 2010 Fifa World Cup to change perceptions of Africa and reposition the continent in a positive light with South Africa as the theatre and Africa the stage.'[10]

'Khoza said the Local Organising Committee had "felt it appropriate that we develop a message, a theme that would resonate with the objectives of the global football family as well as the intentions and ambitions of the African diaspora".'[11]

This is disingenuous and can be easily explained. When Khoza made this statement, it was two months after Jérôme Valcke had written to the South African government on 19 September 2007 to ask that they pay over the money that had been 'promised' to Warner.

It should not be surprising that references to the 'diaspora' payment start appearing in speeches and statements by South Africans at this point. Jack Warner was pressurising Fifa for his money and some way of explaining the payment would have to be developed.

Safa quoted a Bloomberg article in which former President Thabo Mbeki said: 'when we presented our bid to host the 2010 World Cup to the Fifa Executive on May 14, 2004, I said the millions of Africans on the continent and the African diaspora had "embarked on an exciting human journey. This is a journey away from a history of conflict, repression and endemic poverty".'[12]

But this statement was made after 2010 and, curiously, it did not mention the US$10 million that had by now been paid.

Hanging on to this barely credible thread, Safa said: 'We find it quite surprising therefore that the dominant narrative describes the very popular African Renaissance programme's African Diaspora support project as a bribe – almost 4 years after the actual vote to grant South Africa these hosting rights.'[13]

The next leg of Safa's defence summoned up the name of the great South African statesman Nelson Mandela. The association said that Nelson Mandela 'made one of his last foreign trips on 29 April 2004 and visited Trinidad and Tobago to encourage the head of its football association to vote for South Africa to host the 2010 Fifa World Cup. He undertook this 17-hour trip because of his deep desire to fulfill his dream of hosting the world's biggest sporting event in our country.'[14]

'We categorically deny that this was a bribe in return for a vote. It belittles the hard work done by Madiba, Archbishop Tutu, the South African Government and numerous others who sacrificed their time and money and family lives to make our country proud! It tarnishes their images in the most unscrupulous manner.'[15]

But all that this demonstrates is that, as late as April 2004 – two weeks before the Fifa executive vote on the host nation – Jack Warner and his friends were yet to commit themselves to supporting South Africa.

No mention is made of the meeting between Mandela, Mbeki, Warner and Blazer on 14 May 2004, the day before the vote, or of the subsequent smaller meeting with Mbeki after which Warner indicated that he now supported South Africa's bid.

Safa also counts on the complexity of the final arrangement to obfuscate what took place, observing that 'to our knowledge, the South African Government did not make any payment from Government coffers for this project as it was subsequently decided, in a letter written by Dr Danny Jordaan on 10 December 2007 to Fifa, that the money should rather be taken from the LOC budget and then sent directly to Concacaf.'

This highlights another curious aspect of the transaction. Why did government renege on its promise to pay the money? Why was a different arrangement made? Why did Danny Jordaan have to write the letter asking Fifa to deduct the money from the World Cup payment?

Why did Safa's Molefi Oliphant have to write a subsequent letter directing that the money be paid by Fifa and that Jack Warner should control the funds?

Jérôme Valcke clearly understood that Warner was going to be paid by the South African government. In his letter to the then deputy Finance minister, Jabu Moleketi, he stated: 'The South African Government has made a Commitment of 10 million USD to the legacy programme for the Diaspora and specifically the Caribbean Countries.'[16]

Safa's take is that Valcke just got it wrong, that it was 'a fallacy' that government had committed to paying the money.

Safa's spin includes an assault on the US Attorney General's statement that 'the Bid Committee or its representatives approved payments for the purpose of bribery. It was not possible for the 2010 Bid Committee to have made or requested payments to be made in 2007/2008 as has been alleged because it closed shop soon after the awarding of the rights to host the 2010 event in 2004. In other words, the Bid Committee did not exist at the time the alleged bribes were made.'[17]

Again, this is disingenuous. It is quite possible that an undertaking was made while the bid committee was in existence and honoured later by Safa and Fifa.

The fact that Warner left Fifa in disgrace in 2011 following a corruption scandal and the many mentions of his corrupt activities in the US indictment clearly show that this was a man of little principle who would readily solicit a bribe and then demand his money. Safa, though, would have us believe that it was unaware of this side of Warner and that, in its many dealings with him, nothing untoward occurred.

Safa states that Warner's 'position within Fifa and Concacaf at the time made him the ideal candidate to oversee the implementation of the project in the Caribbean'.[18] His subsequent indictment for corruption was apparently a surprise. 'Hindsight always constitutes 20/20 vision,' said the Safa statement.[19]

'The African Diaspora project was – and still is – a genuine expression of both SAFA and the South African Government's desire to position the 2010 Fifa World Cup as a truly African event that provided great benefits to the African continent and the African Diaspora,' the statement continued.[20]

'That the money may have been siphoned off by individuals after it was donated does not make the donor complicit or a co-conspirator as it has been so vigorously described in the public domain,' said the statement.[21]

Mbalula took to Twitter to say the same thing: 'When we organised the World Cup we were dealing with people, not gangsters. The fact that they later turn into gangsters is not our problem.'

The association finished with a threat to journalists to mind their reporting on the bribery scandal, saying it was 'looking at its legal options to counter the deliberate spread of disinformation by individuals that seek to tarnish the only senior Fifa World Cup played on the African continent in the 109 years of Fifa's existence.'[22]

In his only public comment on the allegations, Danny Jordaan said: 'I haven't paid a bribe or taken a bribe from anybody in my life. We don't know who is mentioned there (in the indictment). And I don't want to assume that I am mentioned.'[23]

Jordaan said that under the authority he had in the World Cup regulations – the 'Schedule of Delegated Authority' – 'I could author-ise payments of a maximum of R1m.'[24]

This missed the point, as it is on the record that he wrote to Fifa authorising the payment of US$10 million from monies owed by South Africa to Warner.

'How could we have paid a bribe for votes four years after we had won the bid?' he protested.[25]

This is an intriguing question. Had the South African government promised the money, as Valcke wrote, and then got cold feet, asking Safa to find a way to pay the money via the back door? This would explain the series of letters directing Fifa to deduct the money from that owed to South Africa.

Far more likely, however, is the simple explanation that the money was paid well after the vote in 2004 to avoid the obvious conclusion that it was payment in exchange for the three Concacaf votes.

CHAPTER 10

Fall of the house of Blatter

'I am a mountain goat that keeps going and going and going, I
cannot be stopped, I just keep going.'

– Sepp Blatter

After the completion of the South African World Cup tournament,
Sepp Blatter declared himself pleased beyond his wildest expectations
with the amazing financial return accrued from the hosting of the tournament on African soil for the first time. Fifa's books were healthy,
with a nice US$4 billion in revenue over the four years between 2007
and 2010.

Five years later, a plaster on the side of his face, a spluttering Blatter
was expressing his outrage at being banned from all Fifa activities by
Fifa's ethics committee.

It was an astonishing fall from grace, perhaps the most astonishing
in the history of world sport.

How did this man, who was so powerful that no head of state would
turn down a meeting with him, who could conjure up glistening stadiums where there was nothing or get countries to write laws to exempt
Fifa from tax and other regulatory requirements, end up losing it all?

If there is one person who can be credited with Blatter's downfall, it is the investigative journalist Andrew Jennings. With a mop of long grey hair, a sceptical disposition and a dogged determination not to let the story go, Jennings' persistent efforts led him to uncover how Fifa was turned into a racket.

Jennings cut his teeth investigating organised crime, the Thai heroin trade and the Italian mob before lancing the suppurating boil of corruption on the rear end of the International Olympic Committee. After that, he dedicated himself to uncovering the graft in Fifa, a journey that has lasted 15 years.

In 2006, he published *FOUL! The Secret World of Fifa: Bribes, Vote Rigging and Ticket Scandals*, a classic piece of investigative journalism that revealed the scandalous inner workings of football's leading organisation. Although the book was a popular success, it had no effect on football's elite, who simply stepped up the global network of bribes, backhanders and secret bank accounts that made them rich at the expense of the beautiful game.

Not one to mince his words, Jennings was prone to statements such as 'These scum have stolen the people's sport – they've stolen it, the cynical thieving bastards.'[1]

Perhaps Jennings' bluntness and his passion opened the door for soccer's officialdom to dismiss him. Fifa put out the word that his revelations were the work of a lone crazy. In any event, his exposure of graft sat uncomfortably with many of the embedded sports journalists who flocked about Fifa and its tournaments.

In 2006, Jennings produced a documentary, 'The Beautiful Bung: Corruption and the World Cup', for the BBC's *Panorama* show. The documentary opened with Jennings, camera crew in tow, following Blatter along a sidewalk. Jennings' voice can be heard saying: 'Now this is one of the most unpopular men in world football, and he controls it. His name is Sepp Blatter and his organisation is in a bit of trouble, and I'm another. My name is Andrew Jennings and Mr Blatter can't stand me.'

Then, pressing his microphone in Blatter's face, Jennings asks: 'Let me just ask you this. Do you know which football officials took bribes from the ISL?' Blatter does not respond and Jennings keeps badgering him, asking, 'Why am I banned from Fifa House? What have I done?', before being stopped at a door and then being manhandled.[2]

Jennings may have come across as a rogue, but his posturing was, in fact, part of a canny strategy. His public confrontations with officials such as Blatter were not just showmanship. They were calculated to send a clear signal to the organisation's middle managers that he was on to corruption, hoping that some of them would have a conscience or perhaps a score to settle.

'I've got to get the message to them that I'm here. I'll cross the road for a fight. I want it. I'm looking for it.'[3]

At Blatter's first news conference after being re-elected in 2002, Jennings grabbed the microphone and asked perhaps the most powerful question ever put at a sporting press conference: 'Herr Blatter. Have you ever taken a bribe?'[4]

Jennings recalled the moment in an interview with the *Independent* newspaper: 'Talk about crashing the party. Reporters are moving away from me as if I've just let out the biggest smell since bad food. Well, that's what I wanted. Thank you, idiot reporters. The radar dish on top of my head is spinning around to all these blazers against the wall, saying "Here I am. I'm your boy. I'm not impressed by these tossers. I know what they are. I've done it to the IOC, and I'll do it to them".'[5]

The 'ISL' mentioned in Jennings' questions to Blatter referred to International Sports and Leisure, based in Switzerland, which had the exclusive contract to sell the World Cup, making vast fees from companies putting the World Cup emblem on their 'burgers, sugary drinks and razor blades' as well as selling on very lucrative television rights.[6] In 2001, the organisation had collapsed into bankruptcy, with debts of over £153 million. In a four-year investigation, Swiss fraud investigators unravelled a history of fraud, kickbacks and bribes.

Jennings said in the documentary: 'Why did Fifa give these contracts to ISL rather than to their competitors? Because ISL paid kickbacks, big kickbacks, to some of the men controlling World Football. That's the allegation, but where's the proof? That proof is not easy to come by here in Switzerland. This is still the destination of choice if you've got business dealings you'd rather keep private. That's very convenient for Fifa. The bosses of the world game don't like reporters prying into its finances.'

But pry into their finances he did. 'My investigations only really kicked off when I heard about one secret payment that had gone spectacularly wrong. I was tipped off that an ISL bribe [worth] a million Swiss francs, that's around £400 000, had gone astray. It should have been sent to the private bank account of a very senior Fifa official. By mistake it went to Fifa's account! But when I raised it with Fifa President, Sepp Blatter, a few years ago, he suddenly went all coy.'

Confronting Blatter in Tunis in 2004, Jennings asked about the misplaced transaction: 'It's alleged a secret payment from ISL arrived by accident in Fifa's bank account. Who was it to?' Blatter replied: 'I will not enter into discussion here in this press conference and this is totally out of the matter we like to discuss today.'[7]

Jennings found himself banned from Fifa and from the World Cup.

He followed the money, focusing his attention on the ISL investigation being run by a Swiss liquidator, Thomas Bauer: 'I managed to grab him and I asked him the big question, had he found evidence of bribes. His answer blew me away and I've still got the note of what he said. He told me: "I have found football-related payments from ISL, some are very large, in excess of one million francs. I have written to the recipients asking them to return the money."'[8]

When the *Panorama* documentary aired in 2006, it included allegations that Jack Warner of Concacaf rented his own personal property to the organisation for the princely sum of US$25 000 a month.

Jennings interviewed Mel Brennan, a former official of Concacaf who became disillusioned with corruption in the organisation. He said: 'Well, don't forget, Jack Warner controls 35 votes. He's the swing man regarding votes and voting politics in Fifa.'[9]

In Jennings' words: 'This journalism business is easy, you know. You just find some disgraceful, disgustingly corrupt people and you work on it! You have to. That's what we do. The rest of the media gets far too cosy with them. It's wrong. Your mother told you what was wrong. You know what's wrong. Our job is to investigate, acquire evidence.'[10]

After publishing *FOUL!* he received an intriguing call to attend a secret meeting.

'I go down to London to this anonymous office block, and you go in and there are three men with American accents. They've got government-style haircuts. They introduce themselves as FBI special agents and give me their business cards, which say "organized crime squad".'[11]

Jennings handed over a pile of documents that became the basis of the FBI case against Chuck Blazer, which in turn led to the collapse of the Fifa house of cards.

Reflecting on this years later, he wrote: 'Should a reporter assist the FBI? It was a no-brainer. European police forces had closed their eyes to the huge amount of evidence that I had already published and shown on TV. I was shunned by British football officials, who preferred their privileges gratefully accepted from President Blatter.'[12]

Based on Jennings' documents, the FBI built a case against Blazer. When Blazer was confronted, he decided to cooperate, and this opened the door to a slew of new charges against Warner and others in the upper reaches of Fifa.

The lone quest of an investigative journalist was soon to become the subject of the biggest cross-border criminal case in the history of sport.

* * *

On 20 May 2015, the wheels of the investigation into Fifa began to roll in earnest. In the United States District Court: Eastern District of New York, a 161-page indictment against footballing's elite was filed.

The accused read like a who's who of South, Central and North American football:

- Jeffrey Webb, the man who took over Concacaf from Jack Warner, a Fifa executive committee member and a Fifa vice president;
- Jack Warner;
- Eduardo Li, a former president of the Costa Rica football association;
- Julio Rocha, a former president of the Nicaraguan football association;
- Costas Takkas, a former general secretary of the Cayman Islands football association;
- Eugenio Figueredo, a member of the Fifa executive and a Fifa vice president;
- Rafael Esquivel, president of the Venezuelan soccer federation;
- José Maria Marin, a former president of the Brazil soccer federation;
- Nicolás Leoz, a former president of Conmebol:
- Alejandro Burzaco, head of 'Torneos y Competencias', a sports media and marketing business headquartered in Argentina;
- Aaron Davidson of 'Traffic USA', a company selling football media and marketing rights in the US;
- Hugo Jinkis, head of Full Play Group SA, along with his son, Mariano Jinkis; and
- José Margulies, aka José Lazaro, a 'controlling principal of Valente Corp and Somerton Ltd, companies involved in soccer broadcasting'.

Using the language of the US justice system, Fifa was described as 'the enterprise'.

Jennings had helped get the ball rolling, but why did the US criminal justice system target Fifa with such a high-powered investigation? The answer is that Fifa found itself at the centre of a perfect storm.

After the 9/11 attacks, the US began to ask serious questions about how it was possible for foreign organisations to move funds around its banking system with such alacrity. The movement of cash in and out of US banks through proxy accounts became a major focus for the authorities.

The Fifa transactions started coming out in the wash. They had been laundering money through the US and Caribbean financial systems for years without anyone batting an eyelid. But now they were being noticed and the pile of suspect transactions was growing thicker by the day.

In November 2014, a new front was added to Fifa's perfect storm when President Barack Obama nominated Loretta Lynch to the position of US Attorney General. As US Attorney for the Eastern District of New York back in 2013, she had persuaded Chuck Blazer to cooperate with her local investigation into Fifa.

Obama's nomination came at a time of growing evidence that the criminal justice system was not being fair to black citizens. Lynch's appointment as the 83rd US Attorney General – the first African American woman to hold this position – was confirmed by the US Senate in February 2015. By appointing an African American woman to the post, Obama made a powerful political statement. A perhaps unanticipated by-product was that he had strengthened the hand of someone determined to prosecute Fifa's corrupt elite.

Now Lynch had massive federal resources at her disposal and the Fifa case was elevated to a national priority. The idea was to send a signal to the world that the US financial system was no longer open for business when it came to corrupt 'enterprises'.

Lynch assumed office on 27 April 2015. The Fifa indictment was dated 20 May 2015 – a bare 23 days into her term. The indictment was a searing 161-page account of how Fifa had descended into the mire of corruption thanks to the greed of a few individuals with enough power to reshape the way it did business.

It is no accident that, very prominently, the indictment described Fifa as 'an ongoing organization whose members functioned as a continuing unit for a common purpose of achieving the objectives of the enterprise. The enterprise was engaged in, and its activities affected, interstate and foreign commerce.'[13]

While Fifa's 'principal purpose' was to regulate and promote football across the globe, 'The members of the enterprise, as well as individuals and entities employed by and associated with the enterprise, frequently engaged in banking and investment activities with United States financial institutions.'[14]

The indictment included a detailed description of Fifa's vast bureaucracy. Registered under Swiss law in Zürich, Fifa had 209 subscription-paying member associations representing football in nations or territories around the world. Fifa's highest decision-making body was its congress, composed of member associations.

Each of Fifa's member associations were also members of regional confederations, such as the Union of European Football Associations (UEFA), the Confederation of North, Central American and Caribbean Association Football (Concacaf) and the Confederation of African Football (Caf).

But the real power lay in a much smaller body, one that a few ambitious and unscrupulous officials could control.

This was the 'executive', empowered to take decisions between congresses. It was backed up by a secretariat to deal with administrative matters. The executive had a president elected by congress and members – some of them 'vice presidents' appointed by the regional bodies.

The executive was an all-powerful body responsible for, among other things, 'selecting the host nations of Fifa tournaments, including, among others, the World Cup, the Women's World Cup, the Confederations Cup, the Under-20 World Cup, the Under-20 Women's World Cup, the Under-17 World Cup, the Under-17 Women's World Cup, and the Club World Cup.'[15]

From these tournaments flowed the money that made Fifa's world go round.

'Fifa, the continental confederations, the regional federations and the national member associations often entered into contracts with sports marketing companies to commercialize the media and marketing rights to various soccer events, including the World Cup and other tournaments, World Cup and Olympic qualifiers, friendlies, and other events, as well as other rights associated with the sport.'[16]

The indictment laid the whole corrupt ecosystem bare in riveting detail.

In addition to Blazer, there were several others who, faced with overwhelming evidence of their part in corruption, were now playing ball.

Among them was Daryll Warner, son of Jack Warner, who had sewn up three votes for South Africa. According to the US Attorney General's office,[17] he had pleaded guilty to wire fraud and the illegal structuring of financial transactions.

Warner's other son, Daryan – the man who claimed to have collected US$10 million in stacked bills from a South African official in a Paris hotel on behalf of his father – pleaded guilty to wire fraud conspiracy, money laundering conspiracy and the illegal structuring of financial transactions.

Also cooperating was José Hawilla, Brazilian owner of the Traffic Group, described as a 'sports marketing conglomerate', who pleaded guilty to racketeering conspiracy, wire fraud conspiracy, money laundering conspiracy and the obstruction of justice. Hawilla agreed to hand over US$151 million in illicit money.

Between them, these witnesses had begun to paint a picture of how Fifa had been corrupted, exposing to the world the taxonomy of graft.

At the bottom of the food chain were the plankton of television rights, radio broadcasting rights, advertising rights, sponsorship rights, licensing rights, hospitality rights and ticketing rights, bobbing about on a sea of dollars generated by the viewing public across the globe.

Feeding on the plankton were the fish – the sports marketing companies. They were the ones cutting deals between Fifa and its regional associations, feeding on the money generated by television and sportswear rights.

Feeding on them were the sharks – the administrators who doled out the contracts depending on who paid the biggest bribe or offered the cushiest kickback.

'The revenue generated by the commercialization of the media and marketing rights associated with soccer constituted an essential source of revenue for the enterprise. The United States was an increasingly important

167

and lucrative market for the commercialization of these rights.'[18]

The essence of the indictments was that the co-accused 'together with others, conspired with one another to use their positions within the enterprise to engage in schemes involving the solicitation, offer, acceptance, payment, and receipt of undisclosed and illegal payments, bribes, and kickbacks.'[19]

They had 'corrupted the enterprise by engaging in various criminal activities, including fraud, bribery, and money laundering, in pursuit of personal and commercial gain. The defendants also participated in the corruption of the enterprise by conspiring with and aiding and abetting their co-conspirators in the abuse of their positions of trust and the violation of their fiduciary duties.'[20]

There were the evil deeds, and then, as always, there were the cover-ups.

The defendants and their co-conspirators had 'engaged in conduct designed to prevent the detection of their illegal activities, to conceal the location and ownership of proceeds of those activities, and to promote the carrying on of those activities.'[21]

Every species of corruption was present. There were false 'consulting services' agreements to cover illicit payments. There were artificial contracts. Swarming about these like carrion-crazed seagulls were flocks of bankers, financial advisors and currency dealers inventing shell companies and opening numbered bank accounts in tax havens where questions were not asked about the provenance of sudden wealth. There was active concealment of bank accounts, dodging of reporting on foreign currency, purchase of illicit property and income tax evasion.

Every cent the wrongdoers gained was at the expense of the beautiful game. It was one less cent towards developing the game, improving basic facilities or helping get the next superstar out of the favela and on to the pitch.

The indictment listed the victims: 'national teams, youth leagues, and development programs that rely on financial support from their parent organizations.'[22]

Although a great deal of money flowed towards these corrupt schemes, they actually diminished the financial position of football by 'distorting the market for the commercial rights associated with soccer and undermining the ability of other sports marketing companies to compete for such rights on terms more favorable to the rights holders'.[23]

A key section of the indictment was titled 'Overview of the Racketeering Conspiracy'. It explained how, over 25 years, the defendants 'rose to positions of power and influence in the world of organized soccer', establishing a network of marketing companies 'developed to capitalize on the expanding media market for the sport, particularly in the United States'.[24]

Driven by their corrupt bosses, the organisations meant to govern the sport 'became increasingly intertwined with one another and with the sports marketing companies that enabled them to generate unprecedented profits through the sale of media rights to soccer matches. The corruption of the enterprise arose and flourished in this context.'[25]

Corruption became 'endemic' as the defendants 'amassed significant personal fortunes by defrauding the organizations'.

When found out, they would be expelled or forced to resign, and would be replaced by others promising reform. But, 'rather than repair the harm done to the sport and its institutions, however, these defendants and co-conspirators quickly engaged in the same unlawful practices that had enriched their predecessors.'[26]

One name that kept popping up at the core of the 'corruption of the enterprise' was that of Jack Warner, the man who had swung the vote for the hosting of the 2010 World Cup in South Africa's favour after a very persuasive private meeting with Mandela and Mbeki and a subsequent meeting with Mbeki on the eve of the vote in 2004.

Jack Warner's rise from 1983 until 2011 to a position of power and influence in Fifa, first in the Concacaf region and then globally, when he became a Fifa vice president and a member of its executive, is a key part of the indictment.

In 1983, Warner made his first step when as secretary of the Trinidad and Tobago Football Federation, he became a Concacaf vice president and was appointed to the Fifa executive.

In 1990, Warner was voted president of the Caribbean Football Union and, with the support of Chuck Blazer, was elected president of Concacaf, of which the CFU and Blazer's US Soccer Federation were constituent parts.

Warner reciprocated by appointing Blazer as his general secretary at Concacaf. Blazer moved Concacaf's headquarters to New York, and Warner established the president's office in his home country of Trinidad and Tobago.

The indictment said Warner then opened numerous bank accounts in Trinidad and Tobago where 'he mingled his personal assets and those of Concacaf, CFU and TTFF'. Then Warner and Blazer got to work, soliciting and accepting bribes for the hosting of the 1998 and 2010 World Cups.

Warner diverted funds from the football associations into bank accounts that he controlled for his personal benefit, buying a condominium in Miami in the name of a family member and drawing football money for his own benefit.

There was money to be made from the Concacaf regional competition known as the Gold Cup. The sports marketing company Traffic USA won the rights to five editions of the Gold Cup played between 1996 and 2003. Of course Warner and Blazer needed to be bribed for this to be achieved.

It wasn't always one-way traffic. Other sports marketing companies such as Torneos, controlled by Alejandro Burzaco, and Full Play, run by Hugo and Mariano Jinkis, wanted a piece of the action, and they too coughed up bribes.

A central figure was José Margulies, who was accused of using the Margulies Intermediaries' accounts to move millions of dollars among sports marketing companies: 'Margulies took additional steps to conceal the nature of the payments he was facilitating beyond his use of the US-based accounts. For example, he used the services of currency dealers, he regularly shredded records of his activities, and he discouraged soccer officials who were receiving payments from using accounts in their own names lest they draw attention from law enforcement, though they did not always heed his advice.'[27]

In the five years between March 2003 and March 2008, Margulies was believed to have wired more than US$3.5 million into accounts controlled by other implicated football officials.

The 'Copa América Scheme' promised its participants great riches. Between 1987 and 2011, the sports marketing outfit Traffic USA held the exclusive worldwide rights to the competition after striking a deal with Conmebol – the abbreviation for the Confederación Sudamericana de Fútbol. It goes without saying that this was a mouth-watering deal, with several of the world's top sides – Brazil and Argentina, to name but two – sure to garner a worldwide television audience.

At the centre of these bribes was Conmebol's Colombian president, Nicolás Leoz. His method was a simple one: he looked you in the eye and straight-out demanded money before he would sign a contract.

The indictment records how Leoz gamed the system: 'In a private meeting, Leoz told Co-Conspirator #2, in sum and substance, that Co-Conspirator #2 would make a lot of money from the rights he was acquiring and that Leoz did not think it was fair that he (Leoz) did not also make money. Leoz told Co-Conspirator #2 that he would not sign the contract if Co-Conspirator #2 did not agree to pay him a bribe. After Co-Conspirator #2 agreed to make the payment, Leoz signed the contract. Co-Conspirator #2 caused the payment – a six-figure US dollar payment – to be made to an account designated by Leoz.'[28]

Leoz figured that he should be bribed not once but for each time the tournament was played. 'In approximately 1993 or 1995, the defendant Nicolás Leoz began demanding additional bribe payments around the time each edition of the tournament contemplated by the 1991 Copa América Contract was played.'[29]

And so as the tournament moved from one South American country to another, the plankton, the fish, the sharks and the ravenous seagulls followed, with multiple paydays for doling out the sought-after

commercial rights. Using what the indictment described as 'sophisti-
cated money-laundering techniques', they moved the money around
numbered accounts at Swiss banks using currency dealers to obscure
the source of the money.

Their fatal mistake? They used 'wire facilities and financial institutions located in the United States to make and receive payments'. The
money movements were picked up and investigated.

The indictment listed the dates and amounts of the transactions, all
meticulously recorded by investigators.

Another beneficiary of Traffic's largesse was none other than that
man Warner, after Concacaf granted Traffic the commercial rights to
the Gold Cup tournament: 'Traffic caused hundreds of thousands of
dollars in bribe payments to be made to the defendant Jack Warner
and Co-Conspirator #1 (Blazer), including payments that were made
from or through banks based in the United States.'[30]

Another money pot was the Copa Libertadores, an annual tournament of Latin American club teams that began in 1960. Unsurprisingly,
Nicolás Leoz and others bribed their way to more riches by selling the
rights to this tournament.

Yet another species of corruption was ushered into life in the petri
dish of corruption in which the Brazilian national football team found
itself. After Brazil won the 1994 World Cup, two years of negotiations
around a new sportswear sponsor ensued with the Brazilian Football
Confederation (CBF).

When a deal was finally reached, 'the contract, a 44-page Sponsorship
and Endorsement Agreement, required Sportswear Company A to
pay CBF $160 million over 10 years for the right to be one of CBF's

co-sponsors and to be CBF's exclusive footwear, apparel, accessories, and equipment supplier. CBF remitted a percentage of the value of the payments it received under the Agreement to Traffic Brazil.'[31]

Placing your logo on the famous yellow jersey did not come cheap. A sportswear company – unnamed in the indictment presumably because it was cooperating with investigators – agreed to pay US$160 million for the rights and an extra US$40 million in 'compensation' to the outgoing sponsor: 'On July 14, 1996, three days after the Agreement was signed, a representative of Sportswear Company A and a representative of Traffic Brazil (Co-Conspirator #2) signed a one-page letter agreement acknowledging as follows: "CBF has authorized Traffic, or its designated banking agent, to invoice directly for marketing fees earned upon successful negotiation and performance of the ... [Agreement]."'[32]

Between 1996 and 1999, Traffic charged the sportswear company US$30 million. Half of the money was paid as 'a bribe and kickback'.

World Cup qualifiers were not left untapped by the accused. Home teams had always held the rights to their games, but in 1998, the Caribbean Football Union hit on a new strategy. From now on, the rights to all their members' qualification games would be pooled and managed by the association.

Who was behind this devilishly clever scheme? The CFU's president, Jack Warner, of course. His official duties happened to make him the man 'responsible for negotiating the sale of the CFU member associations' rights with sports marketing companies, including with Traffic USA'.[33]

Warner was not one to miss out on any opportunity for

self-enrichment. He signed off on contract after contract and the illicit money rolled in: 'Rather than paying the full value of CFU's contract to CFU and its member associations, Traffic USA executives, including Co-Conspirator #4, at the defendant Jack Warner's request, diverted a substantial portion of that value to an account controlled by Warner.'[34]

Warner skimmed off the money using his other position as head of the Trinidad and Tobago Football Federation (TTFF).[35] The 2006 World Cup qualifiers serve as a good illustration. Warner put on his CFU hat and sold the rights for US$900000; then he put on his TTFF hat and charged another US$800000 for the same rights he had already sold under the banner of the CFU.

'Upon the defendant Jack Warner's request, Traffic USA executives subsequently wired payments on the TTFF contract to an account at a bank in Trinidad and Tobago that Warner controlled.'[36] Ka-ching!

'Similarly, the 2010 World Cup qualifiers contract provided that Traffic USA was to pay CFU $2.2 million for the media rights covered by the contract, which included the media rights owned by TTFF. At the same time, Traffic USA entered into a contract with TTFF providing that Traffic USA would pay TTFF $800 000 for the same TTFF rights it had purchased as part of its contract with CFU.'[37]

Next in the indictment came the section on South Africa's 2010 World Cup bid, which has been covered earlier in this book. By now, the appearance of the very familiar name of Jack Warner in connection with this 'scheme' came as no surprise.

The indictment does not mince its words. It makes a clear allegation that Warner demanded and received a bribe of US$10 million for three votes from his region for the South African bid.

Then came Warner's big mistake. In March 2011, the Qatari Mohammed bin Hammam, president of the Asian Football Confederation, declared himself a candidate for the Fifa presidency. The other candidate was Sepp Blatter, who was standing for re-election.

Blatter's attention immediately turned to the notorious 'swing vote' of the Caribbean delegates controlled by Jack Warner. Warner's attention immediately turned to how he could fatten his wallet with the dollars that seemed to gush from Bin Hammam's every pore.

Warner agreed to convene a special congress of the CFU member associations to hear Bin Hammam's pitch for the top job. This would, of course, cost a lot of money, so Bin Hammam wired some US$363 537 to an account controlled by Warner via the Bank of America in New York.

The meeting took place on 10 and 11 May at Trinidad and Tobago's Regency Hotel and was attended by the presidents and others from the region's football associations.

Just in case some of those present had not been persuaded by Bin Hammam's speech, Warner put a fail-safe in place. Once Bin Hammam had finished talking, Warner advised the delegates that a 'gift' was available for collection at a conference room in the hotel.

'The officials were instructed by CFU staff members in the room to enter the room one at a time. Inside the room, CFU staff handed each official an envelope bearing the name of the member association that he represented. Inside each envelope was $40 000 in United States currency.'[38]

They were instructed to open the envelope inside the conference room and not to discuss the payment with anyone.

The following day, Warner convened a meeting of the officials and told them that he had advised Bin Hammam to allow CFU staff to distribute the money so that it would not 'even remotely appear that anybody has any obligation for your vote because of what gift you have given them'.

Warner let it be known that he was angry that someone had leaked news of the payment to Blazer, who was in New York.

Then he made an extraordinary statement: 'There are some people here who think they are more pious than thou. If you're pious, open a church, friends. Our business is our business.'[39]

Warner's successor, Jeffrey Webb, was no better. No sooner had he taken office promising to clean house, than he stuck his fingers in the till. According to the indictment, Webb 'solicited from Traffic USA its agreement to pay Webb a $1.1 million bribe in exchange for Webb's agreement to award the 2012 Gold Cup/Champions League Contract to Traffic USA. The defendant Aaron Davidson and Co-Conspirator #2 agreed to the bribe payment.'[40]

The bribe was laundered through a company that made soccer kit and balls.

By the next year, when Webb once again hit Traffic USA for a bribe, his impression of his worth had risen. This time he demanded US$2 million.

All in all, there were 47 counts of money laundering, wire fraud, tax dodging and obstructing justice filed with the grand jury.

There were other incidents not covered by the indictments.

In April 2015, a former vice president of the Egyptian football association, Youssef Harb al-Dahchouri said Warner had hit him for US$7 million to vote for the Egyptian bid for the 2010 World Cup.[41] He told Sada El Balad TV that Warner had asked for bribes in exchange for the Concacaf votes, but the Egyptian government had ruled against any bribe money being paid. Egypt did not receive a single vote from the executive when the selection was made.

* * *

The impact on Fifa of the indictment, the arrests and the endless streams of reporting on the scandal were enormous. It was inevitable that Blatter's Teflon coating would eventually wear through after being vigorously sandpapered by the carpenters of graft.

For years, nothing had stuck to Blatter. In 2002, his then secretary-general, Michel Zen-Ruffinen, accused Blatter of 'financial mismanagement, conflicts of interest and abuse of power',[42] handing over a dossier to the Swiss authorities. Blatter's reputation for evading accountability was enhanced when he suppressed the investigation, saying he needed to preserve the confidentiality of the accused. Blatter survived the ensuing storm of controversy and saw off a challenge for his job by Caf president Issa Hayatou, but Zen-Ruffinen did not and left Fifa.

In 2004, Fifa announced it now had a 'code of ethics'. Blatter would sing the code's praises, saying, 'Since the reforms, we have had an exemplary organisation in ethics. We are the only sports organisation which has this independent body for ethics.' The code placed Fifa 'at the forefront of governance standards in sport'.[43]

The new ethics regime was a classic example of Fifa double-speak. It sounded wonderful but was never given teeth until the arrests of 2015 loosened Blatter's grip on power.

In 2006, the code of ethics had a golden opportunity to strut its stuff. Jack Warner, now a Fifa vice president, was caught with his hands in the cookie jar. He was accused of fraudulently selling tickets to the 2006 World Cup in Germany through a family-owned business. Fifa cleared him, confining itself to expressing 'disapproval' at what he had done.[44] Then it was back to business as usual for Warner and Fifa. Warner kept the US$1 million he was said to have made from the dodgy dealings.

Apparently Fifa's football associations were happy with this weak-wristed regime, and in 2007 Blatter saw off several challengers to secure a third term as president. Among his supporters were the 35 votes coming from Warner's archipelago of island nations in the Caribbean.

An article in *The New York Times* recorded Blatter's increasingly erratic pronouncements. He said there was no racism in soccer and suggested players 'shake hands' and move on if it did occur. He advised gays to 'refrain from any sexual activities' while attending the World Cup in Qatar because homosexuality was illegal there. Women's soccer, he said, would be far more interesting if the players wore 'tighter shorts'.[45]

But Blatter's biggest problem was one of over-reach. The decision to name two World Cup hosts for 2018 and 2022 at the same sitting of the executive opened the door to vote bartering and corruption on a grand scale. When Russia and Qatar, a desert country not renowned for its football, won the two slots, it was too much for many of those who had tolerated Blatter over the years.

After the 27 May 2015 police raids and arrests in Zürich, Blatter's game was up. He won another presidential election, but it was a hollow victory and he knew it. In June he announced that he would call a fresh presidential election and would not stand. In what was perhaps the understatement of the year, he opined that 'Fifa needs a profound restructuring':[46] 'I appreciate and love Fifa more than anything else. And I only want to do the best for Fifa,' he told a media conference. Then, refusing questions, he left the room.

A *New York Times* report attempted to capture the weirdness of the moment: 'After finishing his prepared remarks, Mr Blatter walked off the dais and disappeared through a door without taking questions from the few reporters who were able to attend the speech, which was given on short notice. Mr Blatter's face was grim, a sharp change from the demeanor he showed just days earlier when he brashly responded to a question about resigning with incredulity. "Why would I step down?" he said then. "That would mean I recognise that I did wrong."'[47]

Forced to save face by finally doing something about the graft that had been allowed to carry on under their noses, the Swiss authorities finally acted against Blatter on 25 September 2015, announcing that he faced criminal proceedings over 'suspicion of criminal mismanagement and misappropriation'.[48]

His crimes appear to have been the signing over of World Cup broadcast rights to Warner under dodgy circumstances that were 'unfavourable' to Fifa and an 'unusually large' payment to UEFA boss Michel Platini.[49]

On 2 October 2015, four of Fifa's corporate sponsors – Visa, Coca-Cola, McDonald's and Anheuser-Busch InBev called on him to resign to make way for a reformer who could restore Fifa's credibility. The announcement that Blatter faced criminal charges had finally shaken the sponsors into life. Said Visa in a statement: 'Given the events of last week, it's clear it would be in the best interests of Fifa and the sport for Sepp Blatter to step down immediately.'[50]

Six days later, the Fifa ethics committee banned Blatter, Platini and Valcke for 90 days. Issa Hayatou was appointed interim president.

December would bring fresh trouble for Blatter and Fifa. The Swiss police struck at the Baur au Lac hotel in Zürich, charging more Fifa officials with crimes. The US Attorney General had added more than a dozen new names to its investigation in a new indictment.

Finally, on 21 December, Blatter's career at the apex of world soccer came to an end when he was found guilty of violating the ethics code and banned from all soccer for eight years. For a man in his seventies, the prospect of a comeback is very slim indeed. Platini was also barred for eight years. Both said they would appeal the verdicts. In February 2016, the bans were reduced to six years for both men.

The means-and-ends nation

'We're probably the first government in the world to have taken corruption so seriously.'

– Jacob Zuma

The conventional wisdom holds that the 2010 World Cup represented a massive boost to the South African economy. The argument goes that the infrastructure build created many jobs, that the tourists who flocked to support their teams brought in foreign currency and that South Africa's image as a destination was immeasurably boosted.

The most optimistic estimates usually come from those with a vested interest in portraying the event, in which they were integrally involved as organisers, as a great success.

It seems churlish to attempt to unpick these claims, especially since the World Cup lives on in the memory of most people as a golden moment for the country, one where its many troubles were set aside for a festival of sport.

But a historical record consisting only of praise singing is not of much value. Far more useful is a frank assessment of what happened, the own goals as well as the great strikes.

A truer picture is one of a country capable of great things, but at a great cost. At the heart of all the controversies that beset the World Cup was the replacement of ethical governance with a 'means and ends' attitude, a view that if the end result was a great World Cup, it didn't really matter how you got to the point of putting it on.

Eleven days after the World Cup's final game, the Minister of Finance, Pravin Gordhan, addressed a 'Legacy Dinner' shortly after Nelson Mandela celebrated his 92nd birthday. 'Both the life of Mr Mandela and the hosting of the World Cup share a common thread: the destruction of old myths and the creation of new realities and possibilities,' he said.[1]

The hosting of the World Cup had been 'about the creation of new realities and the destruction of old myths and pessimism about South Africa, and indeed, the rest of Africa.

'There existed a big gap between the old myth of a backward continent where lions roamed freely, and the reality of a country that is as capable as Germany in hosting a World Cup tournament.'[2]

Gordhan went on to say: 'Reporting on South Africa has been the most positive since our successful transition to democracy in 1994. Importantly, for once, South Africans were more optimistic than anyone else in the world, more confident about their abilities than anyone else in the world, and more united about the experience they were creating for both the world and themselves.'[3]

There can be no question that he captured the heady national sentiment of self-congratulation just a few weeks after the tournament came to a close. But he did warn, 'The euphoria we experienced in the past month isn't going to last forever.'[4]

Then Gordhan got down to the economics of the World Cup.

Government had spent R33 billion on hosting the World Cup, which 'acted as a catalyst for expanding our infrastructure base, skills development, employment creation, and economic growth'.[5]

He said the event would add 0.5 percentage points to annual growth for 2010, and if the infrastructure spending since 2006 was taken into account, 'we find that the level of GDP is about one per cent higher than it would have otherwise been'.[6]

Economic projections about the success of a major event are, in any case, usually feats of wild speculation. The actual economic benefit of the World Cup was in fact quite small. Statistics showed that economic growth actually slowed to 3.2 per cent in the second quarter of 2010, when the bulk of the tournament was played, from 4.6 per cent in the first quarter.

The sectors of the economy that grew the fastest had absolutely nothing to do with the tournament. Forestry and fishing grew by 11.6 per cent and manufacturing grew by 6.9 per cent. Sectors that benefited from the World Cup were up, but by much less. Wholesale, retail, motor trade and accommodation rose by 5.8 per cent, while transport, storage and communication rose by 4.5 per cent.[7]

If anything, the 2010 World Cup marked the beginning of a period of economic stagnation. Bereft of large state projects on which to glut their balance sheets, and prevented from colluding, the construction firms found themselves unable to cope with the real economy and began a precipitous decline.

Without the lodestar of a World Cup with real deadlines, government failed to get promised spending on infrastructure out of the starting blocks.

Economist Mike Schussler observed in 2014: 'For the first six months of 2014 construction has declined by 10.2 per cent compared with the first six months of 2013. This decline of over R2.5 billion shows that the construction industry is probably just keeping the wolf from the door. Even more frightening is the fact that R3.5 billion was the decline between the first six months of 2012 and 2013 in real terms. This is the fastest decline in the South African construction industry since 2011 and because it comes on top of so many declines since the recession it is difficult to see how the sector is going to make a turnaround in the short term.'[8]

A further World Cup gain is usually accrued under the column 'social cohesion', a claim that South Africans of all races, genders and social strata got behind the national effort, waved flags together, rode trains together and sat in the stands in the colours of the same national team, blowing vuvuzelas together.

There are several problems with this. For one thing, not all social strata shared in the World Cup festivities. The tickets were priced way out of reach of most people holding low-paid jobs and were certainly not accessible to the unemployed youth. It is not a little ironic that these were the real, week-in-week-out fans who sat in the football stands for domestic fixtures.

There were many football fans in the World Cup stadiums, but they were drawn from the country's booming middle classes. Many did not follow football at all, but wanted to be part of the spectacle. They had the money or, better still, access to the corporate suites where the booze, biltong and cheese puffs were piled high. Driven in and out of venues on luxury coaches, they found themselves in the stands with like-minded people who had also shelled out on the expensive official yellow strip of Bafana Bafana.

Whatever 'social cohesion' occurred in these moments of bonding was quickly undone as the country descended into a quagmire of racial insults on social media, so much so that, by 2016, government began to contemplate a law banning racist name-calling.

Others claimed that the World Cup would provide a boost for local football. World Cup 'legacy projects' included the rolling out of fields and development facilities, and it is too soon to say whether or not these will result in a new generation of footballers taking the national side to new heights. It takes time to develop a child through the school programmes and then through the youth teams and clubs on the route to the national stage.

What is certain, however, is that the national team, Bafana Bafana, slumped once the World Cup was over. After being eliminated in the group stages of the 2010 tournament – for which they automatically qualified, as hosts – they failed to qualify for the 2014 World Cup in Brazil.

They made the quarterfinals of the 2013 Africa Cup of Nations – as hosts – but were eliminated in the group stages of the 2015 event.

By January 2016, Bafana had slumped to 74th in the Fifa rankings and to 17th in Africa. This was a big fall from their 2010 ranking of 51st and an even larger fall from their ranking of 19th when they lifted the Africa Cup of Nations in 1996.

Writing on the 20th anniversary of that famous victory, the soccer journalist Mninawa Ntloko said: 'As much as we would all like to be swept up in the sentimental outpouring of feeling that usually accompanies days like this, it is hard to take a glass-half-full approach to things when the years following 1996 have been so unkind to our football.

'It is hard to allow ourselves to be swept up in the excitement when we know that Rome is burning and the rampaging inferno is threatening to lick up everything in its path.

'Doing that would be something akin to someone with an alcohol problem allowing himself to be consumed by the deceptively comforting fire waters and temporarily forgetting about the mounting bills piling up on the floor. The fact is the climactic euphoria of 1996 was never to be repeated again and there has been a steady decline that continues to this day.'[9]

If there is going to be a '2010 effect' on South African football, it has yet to manifest itself.

In any event, the supposed benefits of the World Cup are overshadowed by the very serious scandals that saw the light of day once the party was over.

Still unresolved is the killing of Mbombela's municipal speaker, Jimmy Mohlala, who blew the whistle on corruption surrounding the construction of that city's World Cup stadium. Between an incompetent local police department and a prosecuting authority caught in the political headlights, there seems very little likelihood that his murder will ever be solved. Until it is, the 18 giraffes that make up the stadium's supporting structure must stand as a silent guard of honour for a man who died for all the wrong reasons.

Two others died in incidents related to the Mbombela stadium build. Would we have built that stadium if we had known that three corpses would be buried before its construction was finished?

The 'means and ends' society would probably answer 'yes'. The ethically correct answer can surely only be 'no'. This was not a battle on the frontline of some war; it was the construction of a football stadium, a facility for sport, for celebration.

There were some consequences for the construction cartel bosses who carved up the World Cup stadium contracts. They had to pay fines to the authorities for rigging the building of almost all of the stadiums and for agreeing on how much money they would make. But were these real consequences? The fines did not exactly dent the balance sheets of these firms.

How much should they have paid? It is difficult to say, but an independent assessment ought to have been done of the amount of money they cost the South African public. What would a competitive bidding process have done to the cost of building the stadiums? What would a profit margin set by the market rather than by executives in a boardroom have been?

All these questions remain unanswered, which is why many of those involved believe themselves to be innocent. They have been allowed to continue with their employment – some even in the same procurement jobs they abused during the scandal. There are many jurisdictions where breaches such as these would be punished with jail sentences for the executives. But in South Africa, the 'means and ends' narrative has produced a curious phenomenon. The wrongdoers are treated with sympathy – after all, they were just doing what it took to get the stadiums built on time. An approach centered on ethical governance would have produced criminal consequences for the individuals responsible.

While the Competition Commission at least brought the collusion out into the open, it should be remembered that laws normally applicable to commercial activity were suspended for World Cup sponsors for the duration of the tournament. That is why South Africans could only purchase Budweiser beer at the stadium concessions. One law, it seems, for local companies and another for those at Fifa's high table. Means and ends.

The scandal of the warm-up matches, which were fixed by referees on the payroll of a betting syndicate, has also demonstrated a failure of ethical governance. Reports by Safa and Fifa officials have detailed how a string of South African officials participated in giving the betting syndicate control of refereeing in the games. A commission of inquiry was proposed by the Sports minister, but the President demurred and it was never appointed. The Hawks have mounted a half-hearted investigation, which has gone nowhere, and not a single criminal charge has resulted.

The only people who have so far suffered any consequences are Lindile Kika and Leslie Sedibe, who were banned by Fifa's ethics committee. (Adeel Carelse and Steve Goddard were also sanctioned.) This means that the officials who colluded with the match-fixers are free to continue with their involvement in football, perhaps emboldened by their impunity.

Fifa has announced a clampdown on match-fixing, but is this likely to succeed if it is to be implemented by member associations that have failed dismally to get their own houses in order?

The most sensational of the scandals – the claim that South Africa rigged the World Cup bidding to obtain the right to host the tournament by paying off Jack Warner in exchange for three votes – is the strongest illustration of the 'means and ends' mentality.

I hope that this book has at least clarified what occurred.

The circumstantial evidence is telling:

- In the weeks leading up to the 15 May 2004 vote on who would host the 2010 World Cup, Jack Warner and his fellow Concacaf officials with voting rights were the only officials who had not made up their minds.

- South Africa campaigned hard to persuade them to back its bid, with Nelson Mandela visiting Warner in Trinidad and Tobago.

- Nelson Mandela and Thabo Mbeki met with Jack Warner and Chuck Blazer on the eve of the vote and then Mbeki held a private meeting with them afterwards.

- After this meeting, Warner indicated that he backed South Africa.

- Warner told Blazer that an amount of US$10 million had been pledged in exchange for the votes.

- Blazer testified in a US court that Warner clearly communicated that the money was a bribe in exchange for voting for South Africa and that he badgered Warner for his share of the money.

- Blazer testified that Warner told him the South African government would no longer pay the money, which would now come from Fifa.

- Safa wrote to Fifa, asking it to deduct the amount from funds due to South Africa for hosting the tournament and to pay it to Warner-controlled accounts, specifying twice in the space of three paragraphs that the money was to be administered by Warner.

- Fifa paid the money over in three separate tranches to disguise the total payment of US$10 million.
- No publicity occurred over the payment of the money, no press release or news conference was held by Warner, Fifa, the South African government or Safa.
- Warner used the money to pay personal loans and to buy himself property, among other abuses.
- Warner paid Blazer US$750000 as a reward for his vote in favour of the South African bid.
- The official South African government book documenting the 2010 World Cup made no mention of the payment.

The kindest interpretation that can be put on this is that Safa naïvely accepted Warner's bona fides and really believed it had to make a massive financial contribution to Caribbean football. And if they voted for South Africa, well, that would be a bonus. It goes without saying that this is very hard to believe.

A far more credible interpretation is that Jack Warner put a price on the votes he controlled, and the 'diaspora' fund was invented as cover for a US$10 million bribe to secure the World Cup. When the government baulked at paying up, Safa came up with a back-door method: getting Fifa to pay out of money owed to South Africa.

If the latter interpretation stands, then you must credit South Africa with some street smarts. No South African signature is on a cheque, no money was paid out of a South African account. There are no South African footprints in the US banking system, which might explain why no South African was indicted by the US Attorney General.

When the news of the scandal broke, South Africans were shocked. But this was soon drowned out by a tide of pragmatic thinking. 'Hey, this is the only way to get the World Cup. It was good for the country, so who cares?' appears to be the stock response of many. The ethical governance response would be to open a criminal case and properly investigate it with a view to rooting out those involved if there was criminal liability. At the very least, some sort of official censure would send the message that such conduct is unacceptable.

But, in the land of no consequences, impunity greases the establishment cogs.

There are still others who question the motives of those who are making the accusation that a bribe occurred. They say that the US, slighted by being passed over in favour of Russia and Qatar for the 2018 and 2022 World Cups, got its revenge by cooking up a plot to attack Fifa. Questioning the political motives of a prosecutor is an old South African trick and, in the land of 'means and ends', it has been used to excuse some very serious crimes.

What this conspiracy theory does not alter are the abundant facts now on the public record, which demonstrate fairly clearly that Fifa was in the grip of a corrupt elite who made private fortunes by illicit means.

Even Fifa's own ethics committee has found that its top officials – including Blatter and Valcke – exceeded the boundaries of decency and has taken action against them.

Back in 2010, I sat in the stands, enthralled by the spectacle and marvelling at the incredible feat that had been accomplished by South Africans. We pulled off a fine World Cup and showed the world that we were a nation capable of greatness. Our government proved that, when the conditions were right, it was capable of delivering as well as the best in the world. Business showed it could come to the party and provide the scale needed for major infrastructure projects. The South African public proved that we were a nation capable of rising above our problems to stand united.

Now, years later, I have my doubts. I feel that we are a great nation, but it's what we are great at that concerns me. We are great illusionists. We can erect a façade as good as any. But behind that façade lurks our true nature. We are a greedy nation, a short-cut nation that takes what it can and hides it well. As well as the best in the world. We are a hollowed-out 'means and ends' nation that has lost its ethical compass. We don't play fair.

Can this be changed? With the right political will, with an independent and dedicated investigative service, with administrators that are ethical or at least prevented by transparency from diverting from an honest path, we could pull it off. But these conditions don't exist at present, and there is no sign that they are about to change.

As long as we are prepared to turn a blind eye to the manifold abuses of public confidence, our football is doomed to languish in the lower rankings and our administrators are likely to place themselves before the beautiful game.

The fate of the key players

Chuck Blazer

In July 2015, Fifa's ethics committee, headed by Hans-Joachim Eckert, banned Blazer from taking part in any football-related activity for life: 'Mr Blazer committed many and various acts of misconduct continuously and repeatedly during his time as an official in different high-ranking and influential positions at Fifa and Concacaf. In his positions as a football official, he was a key player in schemes involving the offer, acceptance, payment and receipt of undisclosed and illegal payments, bribes and kickbacks as well as other money-making schemes.'[1] Among the committee's findings was that Blazer had violated Article 21 of Fifa's ethics code, which prohibits bribery and corruption.

At time of writing, Blazer was suffering from colon cancer.

Jack Warner

Warner was indicted, arrested and charged with 'wire fraud, racketeering and money laundering' in May 2015. In September 2015, he was banned from football for life at both national and international level. He is fighting his extradition to the US to face the charges.

Sepp Blatter

The Swiss Attorney General's office announced criminal proceedings against Blatter in September 2015 for 'criminal mismanagement' and misappropriation.

In October 2015, Fifa's ethics committee banned Blatter from football for eight years following a hearing into a dubious payment to UEFA boss Michel Platini, who was also banned.

In February 2016, the ban was reduced to six years and a new Fifa president was elected.

Jérôme Valcke

Valcke was 'relieved of his duties' in September 2015 and then banned from football for 90 days in October 2015 before being dismissed from the organisation in January 2016.

Danny Jordaan

Danny Jordaan remains president of the South African Football Association and in May 2015 was appointed mayor of Nelson Mandela Bay municipality in the Eastern Cape province.

He did not travel to Zürich for the election of the new Fifa president in February 2016, citing his 'official duties' as mayor. It was speculated that he feared he might be arrested and charged by Swiss authorities.

No investigation has been conducted into his role in the allegations of a bribe payment to secure the 2010 World Cup.

Molefi Oliphant

In 2011, Oliphant was awarded South Africa's highest honour, the Order of Ikhamanga in Gold, 'for his excellent contribution to the development of soccer in South Africa and excellent leadership in the successful bid and hosting of the 2010 Fifa World Cup' by President Jacob Zuma.

No investigation has been conducted into his role in the allegations of a bribe payment to secure the 2010 World Cup.

Tokyo Sexwale

Sexwale stood for the post of Fifa president at the organisation's 2016 election. He did not receive the backing of Safa or the Confederation of African Football (Caf). After making his presentation to delegates, he stunned all by announcing his withdrawal from the race just minutes before voting.

Thabo Mbeki

Mbeki was removed from office by the ruling ANC in October 2008 following a divisive political battle after he fired his deputy, Jacob Zuma, for the latter's link to a corruption conviction.

Mbeki continued to act as an elder statesman in conflict zones and, in 2016, broke his silence on a series of political scandals with a weekly article published online. He refuses to make any public comment on the bribe allegations.

Fikile Mbalula

Mbalula continues to tweet.

Timeline

February 1998: South Africa's bid to host the 2006 World Cup is launched at the Confederation of African Football (Caf) congress in Ouagadougou, Burkina Faso.

March and October 1999: Officials from the 2006 bid committee meet with Charles Dempsey in Auckland, New Zealand, to try to persuade him to support the bid.

August 1999: The official bid document is submitted to Fifa in Zürich.

July 2000: South Africa loses its bid to host the 2006 tournament after Dempsey refuses to vote, handing the tournament to Germany by one vote.

August 2000: Fifa officially adopts the policy of 'rotating' the tournament from one continent to another and decides that the 2010 World Cup will go to an African country.

2001: Fifa affiliate ISL goes bankrupt. At the insolvency hearings, evidence emerges of wide-scale graft and corruption.

2 May 2003: The South African government says it will support the 2010 bid campaign, on its launch in Durban.

26 September 2003: The 2010 bid book is handed to the then Deputy President, Jacob Zuma.

October and November 2003: A Fifa inspection team visits the country to examine its facilities.

May 2004: South Africa comes out tops in the Fifa inspection team's report.

14 May 2004: The 2010 bid committee makes its final presentation to the Fifa executive committee in Zürich. Nelson Mandela and Thabo Mbeki meet with Chuck Blazer and Jack Warner in an effort to persuade them to back the bid.

15 May 2004: Fifa president Sepp Blatter announces 'the 2010 Fifa World Cup will be organised in South Africa'. The nation celebrates.

6 July 2006: The official World Cup emblem is unveiled.

13 July 2006: South African cellular giant MTN becomes the first African World Cup sponsor.

14 September 2007: Celebrations are held to mark 1 000 days to go before kick-off.

19 September 2007: Jérôme Valcke writes to the South African government's Director General of Foreign Affairs, Ayanda Ntsaluba, asking it to honour its promise to pay US$10 million for the 'diaspora' legacy programme. He receives no reply.

November 2007: The 2010 World Cup preliminary draw takes place and the official poster is unveiled.

7 December 2007: Valcke writes to government's deputy Finance minister, Jabu Moleketi, asking 'when the transfer can be done' in reference to the pledge to pay US$10 million to the 'diaspora'.

10 December 2007: Danny Jordaan writes to Valcke to ask that the US$10 million be deducted from Fifa money owed to South Africa and paid to the 'Diaspora Legacy Support Programme'.

4 March 2008: Molefi Oliphant writes to Valcke, insisting twice in the space of four paragraphs that the US$10 million be placed under the 'fiduciary' control of Jack Warner.

2 January 2008: US$616 000 is paid by Fifa to accounts controlled by Jack Warner for the 'diaspora' programme as instructed by South African football officials. Two further amounts of US$1.6 million and US$7 784 000 would be paid later, making up a total of US$10 million.

15 May 2008: 'Host city' posters are launched.

29–30 May 2008: Fifa holds its 58th congress in Sydney, Australia, where the South African organising committee updates it on progress.

22 September 2008: Confederations Cup draw is held and the official 2010 mascot, 'Zakumi', is unveiled.

January 2009: Mbombela City Council speaker, Jimmy Mohlala, is gunned down after exposing corruption around the city's stadium construction.

14–28 June 2009: Confederations Cup is held. Brazil beat South Africa 1–0 in the semifinals, and come back from 2–0 down to beat the USA 3–2 in the final.

4 December 2009: World Cup draw is held.

2 March 2010: Celebration of 100 days to go before kick-off.

29 April 2010: Match-fixer Wilson Raj Perumal writes to Safa, offering to place referees in South Africa's warm-up games. His offer is accepted.

May and June 2010: Referees from a match-fixing syndicate preside over warm-up games involving the South African national team, controlling the number of goals scored to benefit gamblers.

11 June 2010: World Cup kicks off at Soccer City, Johannesburg, with South Africa playing Mexico in a 1–1 draw.

11 July 2010: Spain lifts the World Cup Trophy at Soccer City, after beating the Netherlands 1–0 in a bad-tempered match.

December 2010: Fifa awards the 2018 World Cup to Russia and the 2022 World Cup to Qatar amid accusations of wide-scale bribery.

February 2011: Sepp Blatter approves a payment of 2 million Swiss francs (US$2 million) to UEFA president Michel Platini, which becomes the subject of an investigation several years later.

Fifa's ethics committee bans two officials for wrongdoing linked to the World Cup 2018 and World Cup 2022 bidding campaigns.

May 2011: Fifa suspends presidential candidate Mohammed bin Hammam and Jack Warner after claims they tried to bribe delegates to vote for Bin Hammam.

June 2011: Bin Hammam is banned from all football for life. Warner is not investigated after he resigns.

July 2012: Head of Fifa's ethics committee, Michael Garcia, is entrusted with investigating allegations of corruption in Fifa.

December 2012: Five Safa officials are suspended for alleged involvement with match-fixing in World Cup warm-up games involving Bafana Bafana.

January 2013: The suspension of five officials for alleged match-fixing is reversed.

March 2013: Safa agrees to a three-person commission to investigate the allegations of match-fixing.

May 2013: Former Concacaf executive Chuck Blazer is arrested on bribery charges. Blazer and former Concacaf president Jack Warner are suspended.

November 2013: Jérôme Valcke says Fifa's ethics committee will look into the South African match-fixing scandal.

March 2014: President Jacob Zuma announces that there will be no inquiry into match-fixing in South Africa.

September 2014: Garcia completes his investigation and files a 430-page report with Fifa.

17 October 2014: Fifa announces that the Garcia report into bribery during the 2018 and 2022 World Cup bids cannot be released for legal reasons.

November 2014: Ethics committee chairman Hans-Joachim Eckert publishes a 42-page summary of the Garcia report and says the Russian and Qatari bid victories stand because breaches were minor.

December 2014: Garcia resigns in disgust as Fifa turns down his appeal against Eckert's finding.

27 May 2015: Authorities pounce on 14 Fifa officials at the Baur au Lac hotel in Zürich, charging them with money laundering, wire fraud and obstructing justice. On the same day, Swiss justice officials announce that Fifa executives are being questioned for criminal mismanagement and money laundering.

2 June 2015: Blatter announces that he will call fresh elections to choose a new Fifa president and that he will not stand for re-election.

A letter is published linking Jérôme Valcke to the payment of US$10 million to Jack Warner.

2 June 2015: South Africa's Sports minister, Fikile Mbalula, denies the money was a bribe.

2 June 2015: Former Concacaf official Chuck Blazer says South Africa bribed Jack Warner and himself to vote in favour of the 2010 bid.

7 June 2015: Safa denies it paid a bribe to secure the 2010 World Cup.

16 June 2015: It is revealed that Chuck Blazer worked undercover for the FBI for 18 months while still on Fifa's executive committee.

9 July 2015: Blazer is banned for life from all football activity.

20 July 2015: Comedian Simon Brodkin throws fake money at Sepp Blatter during a press conference.

September 2015: Fifa bans Jack Warner from all football for life.

17 September 2015: Jérôme Valcke is put on leave and released from his Fifa duties until further notice.

25 September 2015: The Swiss Attorney General's office announces criminal proceedings against Sepp Blatter for 'criminal mismanagement and misappropriation'.

8 October 2015: Sepp Blatter, Jérôme Valcke and UEFA president Michel Platini are suspended for 90 days by the Fifa ethics committee.

November 2015: German police search the offices of the German Football Association in connection with deals prior to the 2006 World Cup.

The heads of the German and Brazilian soccer federations resign.

December 2015: Sixteen more Fifa officials are indicted by the US Department of Justice; seven are arrested at a hotel in Zürich.

Former Concacaf president Jeffrey Webb pleads guilty to wire fraud, racketeering and money laundering.

21 December 2015: Blatter and Michel Platini are banned from Fifa activities for eight years after the ethics committee finds irregularities related to the US$2 million payment to Platini.

9 January 2016: Jérôme Valcke is dismissed as Fifa secretary-general.

24 February 2016: Blatter and Platini's bans are reduced to six years by Fifa's appeals committee. Both continue to deny wrongdoing and say they will appeal to the Court of Arbitration for Sport (CAS).

Addendum A: Extract from the US Attorney General's indictment

2010 Fifa World Cup Vote Scheme

185. In or about 2004, the Fifa executive committee considered bids from Morocco, South Africa and Egypt, as well as other nations that withdrew before the vote, to host the 2010 World Cup.

186. Previously, the defendant JACK WARNER and his family had cultivated ties with South African soccer officials in connection with and subsequent to a failed bid by South Africa to host the 2006 World Cup. In the early 2000s, Co-Conspirator #14, a member of WARNER's family, had used WARNER's contacts in South Africa to organise friendly matches for Concacaf teams to play in South Africa. At one point, WARNER also directed Co-Conspirator #14 to fly to Paris, France and accept a brief-case containing bundles of US currency in $10 000 stacks in a hotel room from Co-Conspirator #15, a high-ranking South African bid committee official. Hours after arriving in Paris, Co-Conspirator #14 boarded a return flight and carried the

briefcase back to Trinidad and Tobago, where Co-Conspirator #14 provided it to WARNER.

187. In the months before the selection of the host nation for the 2010 World Cup, which was scheduled to take place in May 2004, the defendant JACK WARNER and Co-Conspirator #1 traveled to Morocco as they had done in 1992, in advance of the voting for the 1988 World Cup host. While in Morocco during the 2004 trip, a representative of the Moroccan bid committee offered to pay $1 million to WARNER in exchange for his agreement to cast his secret ballot on the Fifa executive committee for Morocco to host the 2010 World Cup.

188. Subsequently, Co-Conspirator #1 learned from the defendant JACK WARNER that high-ranking officials of Fifa, the South African government, and the South African bid committee, including Co-Conspirator #16, were prepared to arrange for the government of South Africa to pay $10 million to CFU to 'support the African diaspora.' Co-Conspirator #1 understood the offer to be in exchange for the agreement of WARNER, Co-Conspirator #1, and Co-Conspirator #17 to all vote for South Africa, rather than Morocco, to host the 2010 World Cup. At the same time, Co-Conspirator #17, like WARNER and Co-Conspirator #1, was a Fifa executive committee member. WARNER indicated that he had accepted the offer and told Co-Conspirator #1 that he would give a $1 million portion of the $10 million payment to Co-Conspirator #1.

189. In Fifa's executive committee vote held on May 15, 2004, South Africa was selected over Morocco and Egypt to host the 2010

World Cup. The defendant JACK WARNER, Co-Conspirator #1, and Co-Conspirator #17 indicated that they voted for South Africa.

190. In the months and years after the vote, Co-Conspirator #1 periodically asked WARNER about the status of the $10 million payment.

191. At one point, Co-Conspirator #1 learned that the South Africans were unable to arrange for the payment to be made directly from government funds. Arrangements were thereafter made with Fifa officials to instead have the $10 million sent from Fifa – using funds that would otherwise have gone from Fifa to South Africa to support the World Cup – to CFU.

192. In fact, on January 2, 2008, January 31, 2008 and March 7, 2008, a high-ranking Fifa official caused payments of $616 000, $1 600 000, and $7 784 000 – totaling $10 million – to be wired from a Fifa account in New York, New York, for credit to accounts held in the names of CFU and Concacaf, but controlled by the defendant JACK WARNER, at Republic Bank in Trinidad and Tobago.

193. Soon after receiving these wire transfers, the defendant JACK WARNER caused a substantial portion of the funds to be diverted for his personal use. For example, on January 9, 2008, WARNER directed Republic Bank officials to apply $200 000 of the $616 000 that had been transferred into a CFU account from Fifa one week earlier toward a personal loan account held in his name.

194. The defendant JACK WARNER also diverted a portion of the

funds into his personal accounts by laundering the funds through intermediaries. For example, during the period from January 16, 2008 to March 27, 2008, WARNER caused approximately $1.4 million of the $10 million to be transferred to Individual #1, a Trinidadian businessman whose identity is known to the Grand Jury, and Trinidadian Company A, a large supermarket chain in Trinidad and Tobago controlled by Individual #1. Weeks later, checks totaling approximately the same amount and drawn on an account held in the name of Trinidadian Company B, a real estate and investment company also controlled by Individual #1, were deposited into a bank account held in the name of WARNER and a family member at First Citizens Bank in Trinidad and Tobago. The identities of the Trinidadian Company A and Trinidadian Company B are known to the Grand Jury.

195. During the three years following WARNER's receipt of the $10 million from Fifa, WARNER made three payments to Co-Conspirator #1, totaling over $750 000, in partial payment of the $1 million that WARNER had earlier promised Co-Conspirator #1 as part of the bribe scheme.

196. The first payment, in the amount of $298 500, was made by wire transfer sent on or about December 19, 2008 from an account held in the name of CFU at Republic Bank in Trinidad and Tobago, to a Bank of America correspondent account in New York, New York, for credit to an account controlled by Co-Conspirator #1 at a bank in the Cayman Islands.

197. The second payment, in the amount of $205 000, was made by check drawn on an account held in the name of CFU at Republic

Bank in Trinidad and Tobago. On or about September 27, 2010, Co-Conspirator #1 caused the check to be deposited into his Merrill Lynch brokerage account in New York, New York. Approximately one month earlier, on or about August 23, 2010, WARNER sent an email to Co-Conspirator #1 to advise him that the payment was forthcoming.

198. The third payment, in the amount of $250 000, was made by check drawn on the account held in the name of CFU at Republic Bank in Trinidad and Tobago. The check was delivered to Co-Conspirator #1 by another individual who traveled by airplane from Trinidad and Tobago to JFK International Airport in Queens, New York, and then to Concacaf's headquarters in New York, New York, where he delivered the check to Co-Conspirator #1. A representative of FirstCaribbean International Bank in the Bahamas, where Co-Conspirator #1 held another account, subsequently traveled by airplane to New York, landing at Kennedy Airport. After arriving, the bank representative traveled to New York, New York, where he took custody of the check. He subsequently traveled to the Bahamas and, on or about May 3, 2011, deposited the check into Co-Conspirator #1's account. Approximately two months earlier, on or about March 13, 2011, WARNER sent an email to Co-Conspirator #1 to advise him that the payment was forthcoming.

199. Co-Conspirator #1 never received the balance of the promised $1 million payment.

Addendum B: Safa's Response to Bribery Claims

6 June 2015

This memorandum is in response to requests for clarity from many Safa Members to the announcement of the US Attorney General on Wednesday, 27 May 2015 regarding claims of bribery in relation to the hosting of the 2010 Fifa World Cup in South Africa.

The Association is alarmed by the narrative that has developed around its strong support for the South African Government's inclusion of the African Diaspora in the World Cup legacy projects, specifically in the Caribbean.

Safa joined the South African Government in the fulfilment of this promise to support the diaspora.

We are concerned that the new narrative clearly:

1. Casts the country's inclusion of the African Diaspora as morally wrong, sinister and therefore criminal in nature;

2. Insinuates that leaders in the then Local Organising Committee

and the Government conspired to bribe their way to hosting the 2010 Fifa World Cup in South Africa;

3. Implies that none of the programmes of the 2010 Fifa World Cup were reported and therefore, leaders are trying to cover up their 'misdeeds' by bringing attention to these programmes only now, more than 5 years after the World Cup.

SAFA rejects, with contempt, the attempts to tarnish the image of the country by insinuations that:

1. Support for the African Diaspora programme was wrong;
2. That the African Diaspora programme was not an approved project;
3. That the USD10 million for the African Diaspora was a bribe in exchange for a vote;
4. That somehow there was something sinister with the way we won the hosting rights to the 2010 Fifa World Cup.

On Wednesday, 3 June 2015, the South African Minister of Sport and Recreation, Mr Fikile Mbalula, brought the world's attention to the words of former President Thabo Mbeki, who said the following:

> The basis of South Africa's bid was a resolve to ensure that the 21st century unfolds as a century of growth and development in Africa ... This is not a dream. It is a practical policy ... the successful hosting of the Fifa World Cup in Africa will provide a powerful, irresistible momentum to the African renaissance ... We want, on behalf of our continent, to stage an event that will send ripples of

confidence from the Cape to Cairo – an event that will create social and economic opportunities throughout Africa. We want to ensure that one day, historians will reflect upon the 2010 World Cup as a moment when Africa stood tall and resolutely turned the tide on centuries of poverty and conflict. We want to show that Africa's time has come.

We were also reminded by Minister Mbalula that the African Union views the African Diaspora as one of its 6 regions, the other 5 being on the African continent.

It should therefore come as no surprise that the African Diaspora was included in the benefits of the first Fifa World Cup held on African soil.

The leadership of the bid travelled the world to remind all audiences that the 2010 Fifa World Cup had to benefit the entire African continent in one way or another.

To top these travels, our world icon, the late former State President, Mr Nelson Rolihlahla Mandela, made one of his last foreign trips on 29 April 2004 and visited Trinidad and Tobago to encourage the head of its football association to vote for South Africa to host the 2010 Fifa World Cup. He undertook this 17-hour trip because of his deep desire to fulfil his dream of hosting the world's biggest sporting event in our country.

Madiba's personal diplomacy paid off when Fifa decided to grant this privilege to South Africa. There is no denying the excitement and electricity in the conference room at Fifa when delegates learned that Madiba was present in Zürich to possibly accept the honour of hosting the Fifa World Cup. Who can forget that iconic moment where he held up the World Cup trophy on 15 May 2004?

The presence of the African Diaspora in the programme of the Fifa World Cup is further recognised in the statement of Dr Irvin Khoza, the Chairman of the 2010 Local Organising Committee (the LOC), during the launch of the 2010 Fifa World Cup slogan 'Ke Nako' on 26 November 2007, when he said:

> '"Ke Nako" simply means "It's Time",' Fifa says on its website.
> 'And indeed Africa's time has come to use the 2010 Fifa World Cup
> to change perceptions of Africa and reposition the continent in a
> positive light with South Africa as the theatre and Africa the stage.'
> Khoza said the Local Organising Committee had 'felt it appropriate
> that we develop a message, a theme that would resonate with the
> objectives of the global football family as well as the intentions and
> ambitions of the African diaspora.

Following discussions between Fifa, the 2010 LOC and the South African Government, Fifa wrote to the South African Government on 19 September 2007 outlining its wish that the South African Bid and the 2010 Fifa World Cup Programme should leave a lasting legacy for football and society.

In this letter, Fifa informed the Department of Foreign Affairs of the establishment of the 'Win in Africa with Africa' programme and that Fifa had allocated USD70 million for the programme. Fifa also confirmed in the same letter the South African Government's commitment of USD10 million for the African Diaspora legacy programme, specifically for the Caribbean countries. Fifa also agreed to administer the fund through the Fifa account.

In his recollection of the Diaspora Legacy Programme, former President Thabo Mbeki wrote in an article for Bloomberg a few years after the 2010 Fifa World Cup that:

> when we presented our bid to host the 2010 World Cup to the Fifa Executive on May 14, 2004, I said the millions of Africans on the continent and the African diaspora had 'embarked on an exciting human journey'. This is a journey away from a history of conflict, repression and endemic poverty.

South African foreign policy at the time consciously reached out to the African Diaspora to incorporate them into the African Renaissance that led to the bid to host the Fifa World Cup on African soil.

Fifa itself also always promoted social responsibility and was fully in support of this continental objective, as can be seen from the following story in SouthAfrica.Info:

> In 2004, Fifa announced its vision to 'develop the game, touch the world, build a better future'. The first project to follow from this, 'Win in Africa with Africa' – which is also the slogan for the 2010 Fifa World Cup – aims to ensure that the entire continent benefits from the event in South Africa.
>
> Friday's [7 July 2006] concert also highlighted Fifa's '6 Villages for 2006' charity campaign, which aims to fund the construction of six new SOS Children's Villages in Brazil, Mexico, Nigeria, South

Africa, Ukraine and Vietnam, offering a new home to at least 800 children in need.

– SouthAfrica.Info

We find it quite surprising therefore that the dominant narrative describes the very popular African Renaissance programme's African Diaspora support project as a bribe – almost 4 years after the actual vote to grant South Africa these hosting rights.

We categorically deny that this was a bribe in return for a vote. It belittles the hard work done by Madiba, Archbishop Tutu, the South African Government and numerous others who sacrificed their time and money and family lives to make our country proud! It tarnishes their images in the most unscrupulous manner.

Fifa Executive Committee Members who voted for South Africa in 2004 and who were interviewed by the media at the time all indicated that the tipping point for their support came as a direct result of Madiba's appeal to them as well as the strength of the South African bid.

The '6 Villages for 2006' charity campaign was a legacy of the 2006 Fifa World Cup in Germany and spanned five different continents – and includes South Africa as a beneficiary of one of these projects.

If the bribery logic holds any water, then South Africa may also have been 'bribed' by Germany to support its 2006 Fifa World Cup ambitions upon receiving one of the '6 Villages for 2006'. This was most certainly not the case!

Safa therefore rejects this narrative and restates its support for the African Renaissance and its inclusion of the African Diaspora in the World Cup legacy projects.

We note that the indictment referred to above makes reference to payments made to Concacaf as a direct result of South Africa transferring funds to Fifa to pay this 'bribe'. The indictment notes payments made on 2 January 2008, 31 January 2008 and on 7 March 2008 to the Caribbean Football Union and Concacaf by Fifa.

We concur with Minister Mbalula's statement that, to our knowledge, the South African Government did not make any payment from Government coffers for this project as it was subsequently decided, in a letter written by Dr Danny Jordaan on 10 December 2007 to Fifa, that the money should rather be taken from the LOC budget and then sent directly to Concacaf.

It is a fallacy that any funds were earmarked for Government by Fifa as all agreements and revenue flows pertaining to the Fifa World Cup are signed between the football association and Fifa. Therefore no government funds were spent on managing the 2010 Fifa World Cup beyond the lasting legacy infrastructure that the country's citizens continue to use to this day.

Minister Mbalula also stated that the African Diaspora as well as the African continent benefitted from the 2010 Fifa World Cup African Legacy Programme. In fact, the Safa-Fifa World Cup Legacy Trust still distributes funds to football development programmes around South Africa to this day.

The US Attorney General's indictment infers that the Bid Committee or its representatives approved payments for the purpose of bribery. It was not possible for the 2010 Bid Committee to have made or requested payments to be made in 2007/2008 as has been alleged because it closed shop soon after the awarding of the rights to host the

2010 event in 2004. In other words, the Bid Committee did not exist at the time the alleged bribes were made.

It is also a fact that the 2010 Local Organising Committee, which commenced its work in October 2004, also did not make any payments in the sum alleged in exchange for a vote as it was not in existence during the bidding process. To suggest that this may have happened tarnishes the good names of those hard-working individuals who were selected to serve the LOC because of their impeccable reputations and credentials.

All football associations who participated in the bidding process were required to sign a 170-page Organising Association Agreement (OAA) that outlined strict conditions for participating in the bidding process – including ethical boundaries for campaigning. The following conditions were also placed as irrevocable conditions for bidding:

1. The LOC is and shall remain an internal, fully dependent and controlled division of the host national association;
2. The Organising Association is subject to the control of Fifa;
3. Fifa has the final word on all matters related to the 2010 Fifa World Cup;
4. Fifa does not recognise any third parties or organisations apart from the Organising Association and the Government of the host country.

The condition outlined in the OAA recognises the partnership between Government, the football association and Fifa on all matters pertaining to the Fifa World Cup, including the African Diaspora Programme.

Therefore:

1. Fifa agreed on 19 September 2007 to include the African Diaspora Programme in the 2010 Fifa World Cup Legacy Programme;

2. It was Safa (through its LOC) that wrote a letter to Fifa on 10 December 2007 stipulating how the money should be paid;

3. It was Safa that wrote a letter to Fifa on 4 March 2008 requesting that the funds be managed by the head of Concacaf, whose position within Fifa and Concacaf at the time made him the ideal candidate to oversee the implementation of the project in the Caribbean. Hindsight always constitutes 20/20 vision.

In its quest to host a successful Fifa World Cup, Safa also asked Fifa to assist it in other ways by requesting the following:

1. That it wanted to make a USD100 million profit from the 2010 Fifa World Cup;

2. That it needed USD10 million for the construction of Safa House [granted in 2005];

3. That it wanted USD10 million to prepare Bafana Bafana for the 2010 Fifa World Cup [granted in 2006].

The request to fund the Diaspora Legacy Programme was therefore just one of several requests made to Fifa for assistance.

These requests were made during the hosting period and not during the bidding period and could therefore not be construed as a bribe to someone to vote for South Africa in the bidding process.

It is a shame that this noble effort to support football development has now been turned on its head and camouflaged as a bribe rather than recognising the good that it was intended to deliver to the football programmes of Concacaf.

The African Diaspora project was – and still is – a genuine expression of both SAFA and the South African Government's desire to position the 2010 Fifa World Cup as a truly African event that provided great benefits to the African continent and the African Diaspora.

As noted elsewhere in this statement, Fifa launched its 'Win in Africa with Africa' campaign in 2007. It consisted of the layout of artificial turfs to all African Members of Fifa, training programmes in coaching, administration and refereeing, providing support for Caf's 50th anniversary, developing a DVD on the history of African football, organising a gala match in South Africa in honour of Madiba, etc, etc.

It is common knowledge that many bid committees have previously established legacy and other assistance projects – during the bidding phase – to solicit support from member associations as a means of cultivating goodwill amongst prospective voters. However, the South African Bid Committee did not establish such a programme. Instead, all of its resources were spent on establishing principled relationships with the Fifa voters in an attempt to convince them of the strengths of the country – these strengths were so ably demonstrated during the execution of the 2010 Fifa World Cup.

Minister Mbalula has also outlined the many programmes that the South African Government has embarked on in the African Diaspora as well as on the continent long before the decision was made to bid for the Fifa World Cup. It cannot be correct for these noble efforts to be tarnished in this manner.

221

It is therefore wrong to state that either the 2010 Bid Committee or the 2010 Local Organising Committee agreed or caused these payments to be made to the conspirators referred to in the US Attorney General's indictment referenced above. These matters were dealt with between Fifa and its affiliate, the South African Football Association, in terms of the four key conditions for hosting noted elsewhere in this circular.

To be sure, it was the South African Football Association, after consultation with the South African Government, who requested that Fifa make this grant to the Concacaf confederation – long after the bid was won – to support football development in the Caribbean.

That the money may have been siphoned off by individuals after it was donated does not make the donor complicit or a co-conspirator as it has been so vigorously described in the public domain.

We appeal to all and sundry not to tarnish the intentions of the South African Football Association and the South African Government by deliberate misrepresentation of the facts.

The Association has not been approached by the US authorities to assist in its investigations, but stand [*sic*] ready to do so if called upon as it is in Safa's interest to root out corruption in the sport – wherever this may occur.

We also note the continuing speculation about who are the co-conspirators referenced in the US Attorney General's indictment. It serves no purpose to conduct this trial by media other than to needlessly destroy the integrity of persons who have worked so hard to secure the World Cup hosting rights for this country – without a single shred of evidence being provided so far.

Safa is therefore looking at its legal options to counter the deliberate spread of disinformation by individuals that seeks to tarnish the only senior Fifa World Cup played on the African continent in the 109 years of Fifa's existence.

We thank you kindly for your understanding in this matter and hope that you will be able to defend your Association against the vigorous attempts to rewrite the history of the 2010 Fifa World Cup in South Africa.

Acknowledgements

This book would not have been possible without the support, enthusiasm and guidance of Jeremy Boraine and Jonathan Ball Publishers. The editing and gentle chiding of Alfred LeMaitre once again vastly improved the quality of the final text.

I have to thank soccer fundi Richard Maguire for his help with the final manuscript. Football is not my field of expertise and Richard made up for this weakness with an unerring eye for my mistakes.

Thank you to that writer of excellent prose, Luke Alfred, who gave me advice, contacts and leads that made this a much better book. Likewise, I must thank those doyens of football writing, Bareng-Batho Kortjas (BBK to his legions of fans) and Mninawa Ntloko, who filled in many of the gaps in my narrative whenever I bugged them with my endless stream of questions.

I am grateful to former Fifa security investigator Terry Steans and the former head of referees at Safa, Steve Goddard, who helped me piece together the match-fixing scandal. I also relied heavily on Wilson Raj Perumal's autobiography, *Kelong Kings*, to fill in the gaps in the match-fixing story.

I drew extensively on the reporting of investigative journalists Andrew Jennings, Declan Hill, Mzilikazi wa Afrika and Rob Rose, among others, who have stuck to the job of exposing corruption in football and around the stadium contracts.

Last, but not least, I am grateful to Sylvia and Zoë for once more putting up with my conversion of the house into a book factory and for tolerating my obsessive writing during the December break.

Ray Hartley
March 2016

Notes

Introduction

1 African National Congress, 'Media Transformation, Ownership and Diversity', discussion document, 29 July 2010. Available at www.anc.org.za. Retrieved 19 February 2016.
2 *Ibid.*

Chapter 1: A whistleblower sings

1 All the courtroom quotes in this chapter are taken from a transcript of the sealed proceedings, United States District Court, Eastern District of New York, United States of America against Charles Gordon Blazer, 13-CR-602 (RJD) 13-MC-1011, 25 November 2013.
2 Teri Thompson, Mary Papenfuss, Christian Red and Nathaniel Vinton, 'Soccer Rat! The inside story of how Chuck Blazer, ex-US soccer executive and Fifa bigwig, became a confidential informant for the FBI', *New York Daily News*, 1 November 2014.
3 *Ibid.*

Chapter 2: The 2006 bid: So this is how it works

1 Men's ranking, Fifa.com. Available at www.fifa.com. Retrieved 4 February 2016.
2 Owen Gibson, 'A dark day for Fifa after claims of arms deals for World Cup votes', *The Guardian*, 5 June 2015. Available at www.theguardian.com. Retrieved 22 February 2016.
3 BBC News, 'Dempsey: I was threatened', BBC News, 10 July 2000. Available at bbc.co.uk. Retrieved 22 February 2016.
4 Thomas Kwenaite, 'Bribery claim put Dempsey off', Independent Online,

7 July 2000. Available at iol.co.za. Retrieved 22 February 2016.
5 *Ibid*.
6 Vivek Chaudhary and David Cohen, 'Delegate in World Cup row quits', *The Guardian*, 10 July 2000. Available at www.theguardian.com. Retrieved 22 February 2016.
7 Valencia Talane, 'World Cup's Corruption Blemish', Corruption Watch, 13 June 2014. Available at www.corruptionwatch.org.za. Retrieved 22 February 2016.
8 Andrew Jennings, *The Dirty Game: uncovering the scandal at Fifa*, London, Century, 2015, p 77.
9 *Ibid*, p 79.
10 *Ibid*, p 80.
11 *Ibid*.
12 *Ibid*, p 81.
13 *Ibid*, p 83.
14 *Ibid*, p 84.
15 *Ibid*, p 85.
16 *Ibid*.
17 *Ibid*, p 86.
18 *Ibid*.
19 Spiegel Online International, 'World Cup Scandal: Germany Appears to Have Bought Right to Host 2006 Tournament', *Der Spiegel*, 16 October 2015. Available at www.spiegel.de. Retrieved 22 February 2016.
20 *Ibid*.
21 *Ibid*.
22 *Ibid*.

Chapter 3: 2010: Victory at all costs

1 Inspection Group Report for the 2010 Fifa World Cup, Fifa, April 2004.
2 Letter to Fifa President, Mr Joseph Blatter, Thabo Mbeki, South Africa 2010 Bid Book.
3 Inspection Group Report for the 2010 World Cup, Fifa, April 2004.
4 *Ibid*.
5 *Ibid*.
6 *Ibid*.
7 *Ibid*.
8 Quoted in Njabulo Majola, 'How Mandela's meeting with Jack Warner clinched 2010 Fifa World Cup for South Africa', The News Hub, 5 June

2015. Available at www.the-newshub.com. Retrieved 23 February 2016.

9 Jermaine Craig, 'The quiet meetings that won SA's 2010 bid', Independent Online, 16 May 2004. Available at www.iol.co.za. Retrieved 12 January 2016.

10 *Ibid.*

11 *Ibid.*

12 *Ibid.*

13 *Ibid.*

14 Thabo Mbeki, Presentation to the Fifa Executive Committee on South Africa's bid for the 2010 Soccer World Cup, 14 May 2004.

15 *Ibid.*

16 *Ibid.*

17 *Ibid.*

18 *Ibid.*

19 *Ibid.*

20 *Ibid.*

21 Andrew Donaldson, 'FIFA: Zurich, May 15 2004', *Cape Argus*, 29 May 2015. Available at politicsweb.co.za. Retrieved 1 March 2016.

22 Craig, 'The quiet meetings that won SA's 2010 bid'.

23 Alex Duff, 'Fifa's Warner made late change in World Cup vote, colleague says', Bloomberg Business, 19 June 2015. Available at www.bloomberg. com. Retrieved 23 February 2016.

24 *Ibid.*

25 *Ibid.*

26 *Ibid.*

27 Jere Longman, 'South Africa is named host of 2010 World Cup', *The New York Times*, 16 May 2004.

28 Craig, 'The quiet meetings that won SA's 2010 bid'.

29 Lucky Sindane, 'Decade of a dream', *Mail & Guardian*, 30 May 2008.

30 Longman, 'South Africa is named host of 2010 World Cup'.

31 'Soccer World Cup 2010: Bidding', www.cup2010.info, no date. Available at www.cup2010.info/bidding/bidding.html. Retrieved 22 January 2016.

32 Jamie Jackson, 'The World Cup party Mandela began in Zürich arrives in South Africa', *The Guardian*, 6 December 2009. Available at www. theguardian.com. Retrieved 21 January 2016.

33 Sindane, 'Decade of a dream'.

34 Jackson, 'The World Cup party Mandela began in Zürich arrives in South Africa'.

Chapter 4: What's US$10 million between friends?

1 David Owen, 'Jérôme Valcke: He scored the worst-ever own goal. Now he's running football', *The Independent*, 28 October 2007. Available at www.independent.co.uk. Retrieved 18 January 2016.
2 *Ibid.*
3 *Ibid.*
4 *Ibid.*
5 *Ibid.*
6 Letter from Jérôme Valcke to Ayanda Ntsaluba, 19 September 2007, author's copy.
7 Thabo Mbeki, Address to African Union-African Diaspora Ministerial Conference, 16 November 2007. Available at www.gov.za. Retrieved 6 May 2015.
8 Letter from Danny Jordaan to Jérôme Valcke, 10 December 2007, author's copy.
9 Letter from Molefi Oliphant to Jérôme Valcke, 4 March 2008, author's copy.
10 *Ibid.*
11 Timothy Molobi, 'Oliphant: Danny Jordaan betrayed me', *City Press*, 7 June 2015.
12 *Ibid.*
13 *Ibid.*
14 *Ibid.*
15 'The legacy of the 2010 Fifa World Cup', originally retrieved at www.sa2010.gov.za/en/node/2926, on 17 January 2016. This site appears to have since been taken down.
16 The official website of the Baur au Lac hotel. Available at www.bauraulac.ch. Retrieved 17 January 2016.
17 Owen Gibson and Damien Gayle, 'Fifa officials arrested on corruption charges as World Cup inquiry launched', *The Guardian*, 27 May 2015. Available at www.theguardian.com. Retrieved 17 January 2016.
18 Sport24 and News24, 'Fifa: Who could be Co-Conspirator #15 and #16?', Sport24 and News24, 28 May 2015.
19 US Attorney General's Fifa indictment, DSS:EMN/AH/DAL/SPN/KDE/BDM, 20 May 2015, p 81.
20 *Ibid.*
21 *Ibid,* pp 81–82.
22 *Ibid*, p 82.
23 *Ibid*, pp 82–83.

24 *Ibid*, p 83.
25 Keir Radnedge, 'Julio Grondona approved $10m payment to Jack Warner', *World Soccer*, 2 June 2015.
26 US Attorney General's Fifa indictment, p 83.
27 *Ibid*, p 84.
28 *Ibid*.
29 *Ibid*, pp 84–85.
30 *Ibid*, p 86.
31 Dennis Bloem, 'World Cup 2010: The rot thickens', Politicsweb, 7 June 2015. Available at politicsweb.co.za. Retrieved 24 February 2016.
32 *Ibid*.
33 Fifa, 'Fédération Internationale de Football Association's Victim Statement and Request for Restitution', 15 March 2016, p 10
34 *Ibid*.
35 *Ibid*.
36 Peter Pedroncelli, 'FIFA Explains South African World Cup Restitution Claim', AFK Sports, 22 March 2016.

Chapter 5: What a carve-up

1 Collette Schulz Herzenberg (ed.), *Player and Referee: Conflicting Interests and the 2010 Fifa World Cup*, Pretoria, Institute for Security Studies, 2010, p 11.
2 *Ibid*, p 5.
3 Karen Schoonbee and Stefaans Brümmer, 'Public loss, Fifa's gain: How Cape Town got its white elephant', in Herzenberg (ed.), *Player and Referee*, p 139.
4 *Ibid*, p 134.
5 *Ibid*, p 142.
6 Regulations cited in Schoonbee and Brümmer, 'Public loss, Fifa's gain', p 138.
7 Cited in Schoonbee and Brümmer, 'Public loss, Fifa's gain', p 146.
8 City of Cape Town, 'Cape Town Stadium', webpage, 2009. Available at www.capetown.gov.za/en/Fifa2010/Pages/CapeTownStadium.aspx. Retrieved 25 February 2016.
9 Quoted in Eddie Botha and Gcina Ntsaluba, 'Tendering irregularities in the Eastern Cape', in Herzenberg (ed.), *Player and Referee*, p 53.
10 Quoted in Sam Sole, 'Durban's Moses Mabhida Stadium', in Herzenberg (ed.), *Player and Referee*, p 176.
11 Mike Sutcliffe, 'City Manager's Newsletter', undated. Available at www.durban.gov.za. Retrieved 8 March 2016.

12 *Ibid.*
13 Sole, 'Durban's Moses Mabhida Stadium', p 177.
14 Rob Rose, 'Soccer City: What it says about the murky world of government tenders', in Herzenberg (ed.), *Player and Referee*, p 40.
15 *Ibid.*
16 *Ibid.*
17 *Ibid*, p 41.
18 *Ibid.*
19 *Ibid*, p 35.
20 *Ibid*, p 35.
21 *Ibid*, p 36.
22 Founding affidavit, Fhatuwani Elphus Mudimeli, CC CASE NO: 2009Feb4279, p. 10.
23 *Ibid.*
24 *Ibid*, p 11.
25 *Ibid*, p 14.
26 *Ibid*, p 7.
27 *Ibid*, p 14.
28 *Ibid*, p 15.
29 Competition Commission of South Africa, 'Construction firms settle collusive tendering case for R1.5bn in penalties', media release, 24 June 2013.
30 'Construction cartel hearings: Not a great day for transparency', *City Press*, 21 July 2013. Available at www.news24.com. Retrieved 29 April 2015.
31 *Ibid.*
32 *Ibid.*
33 *Ibid.*
34 *Ibid.*
35 *Ibid.*
36 *Ibid.*
37 Henry Laas, '"We're sorry," says Murray & Roberts CEO Henry Laas', *Business Times*, re-published on bdlive.co.za, 21 July 2013. Retrieved 25 February 2016.
38 *Ibid.*
39 *Ibid.*
40 City of Cape Town, 'Business Plan for Cape Town Stadium and Green Point Park', public information summary and report, City of Cape Town, 2012, p 6.

Chapter 6: The fix is in

1 Wilson Raj Perumal, 'RE: REFEREES EXCHANGE PROGRAM', letter, 29 April 2010.
2 Declan Hill and Jere Longman, 'Fixed soccer matches cast shadow over World Cup', *The New York Times*, 31 May 2014. Available at www.nyt. com. Retrieved 6 October 2015.
3 Don Riddell and Matthew Knight, 'Wilson Raj Perumal: The man who fixed football', CNN, 26 August 2014. Available at cnn.com. Retrieved 26 February 2016.
4 *Ibid.*
5 Wilson Raj Perumal with Alessandro Righi and Emanuele Piano, *Kelong Kings: Confessions of the world's most prolific match-fixer*, self-published, Amazon Kindle edition, location 2622 and 2014.
6 *Ibid.*
7 *Ibid.*
8 *Ibid.*
9 *Ibid*, location 2641.
10 *Ibid*, location 2661.
11 *Ibid*, location 2701.
12 *Ibid*, location 2701.
13 Riddell and Knight, 'Wilson Raj Perumal'.
14 Interpol, 'Match-fixing in Football – Training Needs Assessment', report, 14 August 2013, p 13.
15 Perumal, *Kelong Kings*, location 6074.
16 Author's interview with Steve Goddard, 3 March 2016.
17 Perumal, *Kelong Kings*, location 6112.
18 *Ibid.*
19 'Agreement' document signed by Leslie Sedibe on 11 May 2010.
20 *Ibid.*
21 Perumal, *Kelong Kings*, location 6132.
22 *Ibid*, location 6282.
23 *Ibid.*
24 Declan Hill, 'The fixers and the officials', PlaytheGame, 16 June 2014. Available at www.playthegame.org. Retrieved 6 October 2015.
25 Author's interview with Steve Goddard, 3 March 2016.
26 Perumal, *Kelong Kings*, location 6409.
27 *Ibid*, location 6410.
28 Author's interview with Steve Goddard, 3 March 2016.
29 Perumal, *Kelong Kings*, location 6448.

30 *Ibid*, location 6469.
31 Hill and Longman, 'Fixed soccer matches cast shadow over World Cup'.
32 Hill, 'The fixers and the officials'.
33 *Ibid*.
34 Fifa Security Department, 'Allegations of impropriety against some employees of the South African Football Association and other individuals in some pre-World Cup 2010 international friendly matches', report by Terry Steans, 4 October 2012, p 5.
35 *Ibid*.
36 *Ibid*, p 6.
37 *Ibid*.
38 *Ibid*.
39 *Ibid*, p 8.
40 *Ibid*, pp 10–11.
41 *Ibid*, p 11.
42 *Ibid*, p 35.
43 *Ibid*, p 23.
44 *Ibid*, p 24.
45 *Ibid*, p 22.
46 *Ibid*.
47 *Ibid*, p 27.
48 *Ibid*, p 32.
49 *Ibid*, p 33.
50 *Ibid*, p 25.
51 *Ibid*, p 29.
52 *Ibid*, p 30.
53 *Ibid*, p 42.
54 *Ibid*, p 43.
55 *Ibid*, p 44.
56 Fifa, 'Judicial commission of enquiry to be mandated in South Africa', Fifa media release, 5 April 2013.
57 *Ibid*.
58 *Ibid*.
59 *Ibid*.
60 Hill, 'The fixers and the officials'.
61 Mninawa Ntloko, 'Mbalula shock over Zuma's no to match fixing probe', *Sunday Times*, 9 March 2014.
62 Fifa, 'Independent Ethics Committee suspends Lindile Kika from all footballing activity for six years', media release, 14 October 2015.
63 Author's interview with Steve Goddard, 3 March 2016.

64 *Ibid.*
65 'Response to the Fifa sanction against Leslie Sedibe', press release, 14 March 2016.
66 *Ibid.*
67 *Ibid.*
68 Mazola Molefe and Mninawa Ntloko, 'Safa stunned by Kika ban', *Sowetan*, 15 October 2015.
69 Author's correspondence with Terry Steans, 3 March 2016.
70 *Ibid.*
71 *Ibid.*
72 Andy Brown, 'Wilson Raj Perumal fixed 2010 World Cup qualification', The Sports Integrity Initiative, 24 February 2015. Available at www. sportsintegrityinitiative.com. Retrieved 26 February 2016.
73 *Ibid.*
74 Riddell and Knight, 'Wilson Raj Perumal'.
75 Interpol, 'Match-fixing in Football', p 11.
76 *Ibid*, p 14.

Chapter 7: Where the bodies are buried

1 Hugh Sykes, 'Stink of scandal from South Africa's giraffe stadium', BBC News, 7 June 2010.
2 Mzilikazi wa Afrika, *Nothing Left to Steal*, Johannesburg, Penguin, 2014.
3 Mbombela Local Municipality, 'Mbombela Stadium Facts – Africa's Wildest Stadium', undated article. Available at www.mbombela.gov.za. Retrieved 26 February 2016.
4 Fifa, '"Africa's wildest stadium" set to illuminate World Cup', Fifa (LOC) media release, 29 September 2009. Available at www.fifa.com. Retrieved 26 February 2016.
5 *Ibid.*
6 Calculated on exchange rates in February 2016.
7 Brian Spilg, SC, 'The fight for land – round two (asset grabbing)', *Advocate*, April 2009, p 42.
8 'Scandals, murder taint World Cup stadium', Reuters, 27 October 2009. Available at www.reuters.com. Retrieved 7 March 2016.
9 *Ibid.*
10 Sydney Masinga and Justin Arenstein, 'The three years leading to Jimmy Mohlala's death', Ziwaphi Online, 18 April 2015. Available at ziwaphi. com. Retrieved 26 February 2016.
11 *Ibid.*

12 *Ibid.*
13 Lucky Sindane, 'ANC in stadium cover up', *Mail & Guardian*, 22 February 2009.
14 *Ibid.*
15 *Ibid.* The French multinational Bouygues is the majority shareholder in Basil Read.
16 Masinga and Arenstein, 'The three years leading to Jimmy Mohlala's death'.
17 'Mbombela Stadium corruption: Hawks make arrests', *City Press*, 15 August 2012. Available at www.news24.com. Retrieved 26 February 2016.
18 'Mbombela Stadium fraud case on hold', News24, 15 October 2012. Available at www.news24.com. Retrieved 26 February 2016.
19 Omphitlhetse Mooki and Piet Rampedi, 'Kaizer Chiefs boss held for tender fraud', *The Star*, 16 August 2012.
20 Masinga and Arenstein, 'The three years leading to Jimmy Mohlala's death.
21 'Mbombela Stadium fraud case on hold'.
22 'Mbombela Stadium corruption: Hawks make arrests'.
23 Alfred Moselakgomo, 'Dladla is guilty', *Sowetan*, 24 June 2009.
24 'Mbombela Stadium corruption: Hawks make arrests'.
25 Sykes, 'Stink of scandal from South Africa's giraffe stadium'.
26 Mooki and Rampedi, 'Kaizer Chiefs boss held for tender fraud'.
27 Abram Mashego and Sizwe Sama Yende, 'Bobby Motaung to face the music', *City Press*, 24 January 2016.

Chapter 8: A nation transfixed

1 Department of Sport and Recreation, '2010 Fifa World Cup Country Report', p 69. Available at www.srsa.gov.za. Retrieved 29 February 2016.
2 Janine Erasmus, 'Rhythm, colour at the World Cup concert', Southafrica.info, 11 June 2010. Available at www.southafrica.info. Retrieved 19 September 2015.
3 Department of Sport and Recreation, '2010 Fifa World Cup Country Report', p 69.
4 SAinfo, '2010 World Cup tickets now on sale', 20 February 2009. Available at www.southafrica.info. Retrieved 9 March 2016.
5 Robin Bairner, 'World Cup 2010: Fifa President Sepp Blatter & South Africa President Jacob Zuma declare tournament open and hail Nelson Mandela', Goal.com, 11 June 2010. Available at www.goal.com.

Retrieved 21 January 2016.
6 *Ibid.*
7 Department of Sport and Recreation, '2010 Fifa World Cup Country Report', p 10.
8 *Ibid*, p 17.
9 *Ibid.*
10 *Ibid*, p 18.
11 *Ibid*, p 19.
12 *Ibid*, pp 19–20.
13 *Ibid*, p 53.
14 *Ibid*, p 23.
15 *Ibid*, p 21.
16 *Ibid*, p 34.
17 *Ibid*, p 21.
18 *Ibid*, p 26.
19 *Ibid*, p 24.
20 *Ibid*, p 25.
21 *Ibid*, p 26.
22 *Ibid*, p 30.
23 *Ibid*, p 31.
24 *Ibid*, p 32.
25 *Ibid*, p 33.
26 *Ibid*, p 38.
27 *Ibid.*
28 *Ibid*, p 41.
29 *Ibid*, p 43.
30 *Ibid*, p 76.
31 Quoted in *El Periodico de Catalunya*, original source not available. Available at en.wikipedia.org/wiki/2010_Fifa_World_Cup_Final. Retrieved 20 January 2016.
32 Fifa, 'Fifa Financial Report 2010', 31 May and 1 June 2011, p 7.
33 *Ibid*, p 16.
34 Sepp Blatter, 'Looking back and forwards', *Fifa World*, April 2011, p 12.
35 Department of Sport and Recreation, '2010 Fifa World Cup Country Report', p 98.
36 *Ibid*, p 4.
37 *Ibid*, p 5.
38 *Ibid*, p 22.
39 *Ibid*, p 10.
40 *Ibid*, p 98.

Chapter 9: Spinning out of control

1 Author's correspondence with the office of former President Thabo Mbeki, 1 March 2016.
2 Author's correspondence with the office of Danny Jordaan, 3 March 2016.
3 *Ibid.*
4 Adam Wakefield, 'Don't speculate about 2010 bribe individuals – Mbalula', News24, 31 May 2015. Available at www.news24.com. Retrieved 29 February 2016.
5 *Ibid.*
6 South African Football Association, 'SAFA's response to bribery claims', *SAFA News*, 6 June 2015. Available at www.safa.net. Retrieved 29 February 2016.
7 *Ibid.*
8 Department of Sport and Recreation, '2010 Fifa World Cup Country Report', p 4.
9 South African Football Association, 'SAFA's response to bribery claims'.
10 *Ibid.*
11 *Ibid.*
12 *Ibid.*
13 *Ibid.*
14 *Ibid.*
15 *Ibid.*
16 RDM Staff, 'Fifa man's letters to SA government about US10m bribe – full text', Rand Daily Mail, 8 June 2015. Available at www.rdm.co.za. Retrieved 29 February 2016.
17 South African Football Association, 'SAFA's response to bribery claims'.
18 *Ibid.*
19 *Ibid.*
20 *Ibid.*
21 *Ibid.*
22 *Ibid.*
23 eNCA, 'Jordaan knew about $10m, but denies bribery', eNCA, 1 June 2015, Available at enca.com. Retrieved 29 February 2016.
24 *Ibid.*
25 *Ibid.*

Chapter 10: Fall of the house of Blatter

1 Michael E Miller, 'Andrew Jennings: Meet the man that exposed the Fifa

scandal that toppled Sepp Blatter', *Independent*, 3 June 2015.

2 BBC, 'The Beautiful Bung: Corruption and the World Cup', transcript recorded from transmission, 13 June 2006. Available at www.bbc.co.uk. Retrieved 20 January 2016.

3 Michael E Miller, 'Andrew Jennings'.

4 *Ibid.*

5 *Ibid.*

6 BBC, 'The Beautiful Bung'.

7 *Ibid.*

8 *Ibid.*

9 *Ibid.*

10 Michael E Miller, 'Andrew Jennings'.

11 *Ibid.*

12 Jennings, *The Dirty Game*, p 3.

13 United States of America, Indictment 15 CR 0252 (RJD) (RML), 20 May 2015, p 2.

14 *Ibid.*

15 *Ibid*, p 5.

16 *Ibid*, p 13.

17 United States Department of Justice, 'Nine Fifa Officials and Five Corporate Executives Indicted for Racketeering Conspiracy and Corruption', press release, Office of Public Affairs, US Department of Justice, 27 May 2015.

18 United States of America, Indictment 15 CR 0252 (RJD) (RML), p 14.

19 *Ibid*, p 29.

20 *Ibid.*

21 *Ibid.*

22 *Ibid*, p 30.

23 *Ibid*, pp 30–31

24 *Ibid*, p 31.

25 *Ibid.*

26 *Ibid.*

27 *Ibid*, p 39.

28 *Ibid*, p 50.

29 *Ibid.*

30 *Ibid*, p 62.

31 *Ibid*, p 75.

32 *Ibid.*

33 *Ibid*, p 77.

34 *Ibid*, p 78.

35 Renamed the Trinidad and Tobago Football Association (TTFA) in 2013.
36 United States of America, Indictment 15 CR 025 (RJD) (RML), p 79.
37 *Ibid*, pp 79–80.
38 *Ibid*, pp 91–92.
39 *Ibid*.
40 *Ibid*, pp 99–100.
41 'Fifa accused of asking for bribe to support Egypt's bid for 2010 Soccer World Cup', Morocco World News, 21 April 2015.
42 *The New York Times*, 'The rise and fall of Sepp Blatter', timeline, *The New York Times*, 21 December 2015.
43 Sky Sports, 'Ethics investigator, Michael Garcia, says Fifa must be more open', SkySports.com, 20 September 2014.
44 *The New York Times*, 'The rise and fall of Sepp Blatter'.
45 *Ibid*.
46 *Ibid*.
47 Sam Borden, Michael S Schmidt and Matt Apuzo, 'Sepp Blatter decides to resign as Fifa president in about face', *The New York Times*, 2 June 2015.
48 *The New York Times*, 'The rise and fall of Sepp Blatter'.
49 *Ibid*.
50 Andrew Das, 'Coca-Cola, Visa, McDonald's and Anheuser-Busch call on Fifa's Sepp Blatter to resign', *The New York Times*, 2 October 2015.

Conclusion: The means-and-ends nation

1 Pravin Gordhan, 'South Africa's Infrastructure and Legacy After the 2010 Fifa World Cup and What It Means for an Emerging Economy', speech to *Financial Times* Future and Legacy Dinner, 22 July 2010, p 2.
2 *Ibid*, pp 2–3.
3 *Ibid*, p 3.
4 *Ibid*, p 2.
5 *Ibid*, p 4.
6 *Ibid*.
7 KPMG, *Economic Insight, Quarterly Review*, Quarter 3 2010, Issue 13, p 2.
8 Mike Schussler, 'A quick and massive decline in construction', Moneyweb, 27 August 2014.
9 Mninawa Ntloko, 'Africa Cup of Nations glory – then 20 years of failure', Rand Daily Mail, 3 February 2016. Available at rdm.co.za. Retrieved 29 February 2016.

The fate of the key players

1 Fifa, 'Independent Ethics Committee bans Chuck Blazer from football related activities for life', Fifa media release, 9 July 2015.

References

Selected books, reports, letters and speeches

African National Congress, 'Media Transformation, Ownership and Diversity', ANC discussion document, 29 July 2010. Available from www.anc.org.za. Retrieved 19 February 2016.

City of Cape Town, 'Business Plan for Cape Town Stadium and Green Point Park', public information summary and report, City of Cape Town, 2012.

Department of Sport and Recreation, '2010 Fifa World Cup Country Report'. Available at www.srsa.gov.za. Retrieved 29 February 2016.

Fifa, 'Fifa Financial Report 2010', 31 May and 1 June 2011.

Fifa Security Department, 'Allegations of impropriety against some employees of the South African Football Association and other individuals in some pre-World Cup 2010 international friendly matches', report by Terry Steans, 4 October 2012.

Founding Affidavit, Fhatuwani Elphus Mudimeli, CC CASE NO: 2009Feb4279.

Herzenberg, Collette Schulz (ed.), *Player and Referee: Conflicting interests and the 2010 Fifa World Cup*, Pretoria, Institute for Security Studies, 2010.

Inspection Group Report for the 2010 Fifa World Cup, Fifa, April 2004.

Interpol, 'Match-fixing in Football – Training Needs Assessment', report, 14 August 2013.

Jennings, Andrew, *FOUL! The Secret World of Fifa: Bribes, Vote Rigging and Ticket Scandals*, London, HarperSport, 2008.

Jennings, Andrew, *The Dirty Game: Uncovering the scandal at Fifa*, London, Century, 2015.

Letter from Danny Jordaan to Jérôme Valcke, 10 December 2007.

Letter from Molefi Oliphant to Jérôme Valcke, 4 March 2008.

Perumal, Wilson Raj with Alessandro Righi and Emanuele Piano, *Kelong Kings: Confessions of the world's most prolific match-fixer*, Kindle edition, 2014.

Pravin Gordhan, 'South Africa's infrastructure and legacy after the 2010 Fifa World Cup and what it means for an emerging economy', speech to *Financial Times* Future and Legacy Dinner, 22 July 2010.

South African Football Association, 'SAFA's response to bribery claims', *SAFA News*, 6 June 2015.

Thabo Mbeki, Address to African Union-African Diaspora Ministerial Conference, 16 November 2007.

Thabo Mbeki, Letter to Fifa President, Mr Joseph Blatter, South Africa 2010 Bid Book.

Thabo Mbeki, Presentation to the Fifa Executive Committee on South Africa's bid for the 2010 Soccer World Cup, 14 May 2004.

Transcript of the sealed proceedings, United States District Court, Eastern District of New York, United States of America against Charles Gordon Blazer, 13-CR-602 (RJD) 13-MC-1011, 25 November 2013.

United States of America, Indictment 15 CR 0252 (RJD) (RML), 20 May 2015.

US Attorney General's FIFA indictment, DSS:EMN/AH/DAL/SPN/KDE/BDM, 20 May 2015.

Wa Afrika, Mzilikazi, *Nothing Left to Steal*, Johannesburg, Penguin, 2014.

Index